What people are sa

Energy Magick

Mark and I have been good friends for quite a few years, so I was pleased to receive and read his first book—a comprehensive manual for a wide range of energy magick, both introductory and advanced. All of the exercises and practices are designed to be done by the individual practitioner, and they are all based on visualization techniques he presents in the first chapters. No physical tools, candles, herbs, statues, altars or special regalia are required—only a disciplined mind. Straightforward practical instructions and easy-to-follow progressive step-by-step exercises teach creating sacred space, grounding, centering, meditation, healing and cord-cutting. Detailed information with tables and diagrams cover chakras, auras, energy bodies, runes and sigils, and astrological correspondences.

The later section on advanced energy work provides complete instructions and practical exercises for astral projection, shielding, setting wards, Shadow work, trance journeying, evocation and invocation, creating egregores, spellwork and ritual. The final section is a concise Grimoire covering offensive and defensive magick, spellwork for protection, prosperity, success, empowerment, and personal spiritual evolution.

No magickal library is complete without this practical workbook on energy magick. It is a valuable resource you will return to frequently.

Oberon Zell, author of *Grimoire for the Apprentice Wizard,* and *GaeaGenesis: Conception and Birth of the Living Earth*

Energy Magick is a refreshingly straightforward primer on all the important aspects of magical work which are too often glossed over or rushed through. This book will walk you through understanding what magical energy work is and how

to do it for any purpose, from daily essentials like grounding to advanced work including shapeshifting and breaking curses. A must have for any witch or magical practitioner.
Morgan Daimler, author of *Fairycraft* and *Travelling the Fairy Path*

All witches need to be able to manipulate magical energy. It's a fundamental skill taught in all good covens as basic training, but if you're a solitary practitioner learning on your own, you're likely to need help. *Energy Magick* by Mark NeCamp, Jr. is the perfect guide – an instruction manual for all kinds of magical energy work from grounding through to invocation and evocation. It explains what these forces are, how they work, and how you can learn to sense and manipulate them. At each step of the way there are practical exercises. The book is in two sections: basic energy work, and advanced techniques. If you're a complete beginner I'd recommend working your way through everything. If you're more experienced, skim the early stuff as a refresher, then go on to section two. This should be an essential text for any trainee in the magical arts. The book is well written, concise and packed with useful information.
Lucya Starza, author of *Candle Magic, Poppets and Magical Dolls, Guided Visualizations, Scrying,* and *The Wheel of the Year*

NeCamp's excellent book cuts through the fat of traditional spellwork and shows the reader how to perform magick directly, without the cumbersome tools that can be intimidating and cost prohibitive to the beginner. *Energy Magick* is a valuable resource for practitioners of all skill levels.
Logan Albright, author of *Libertarian Paganism* and *Conform or Be Cast Out: The (Literal) Demonization of Nonconformists*

Energy Magick

A Basic & Advanced Guide
for Witches & Pagans

Energy Magick

A Basic & Advanced Guide for Witches & Pagans

Mark NeCamp, Jr.

**MOON
BOOKS**

Winchester, UK
Washington, USA

JOHN HUNT PUBLISHING

First published by Moon Books, 2024
Moon Books is an imprint of John Hunt Publishing Ltd., No. 3 East Street, Alresford
Hampshire SO24 9EE, UK
office@jhpbooks.net
www.johnhuntpublishing.com
www.moon-books.net

For distributor details and how to order please visit the 'Ordering' section on our website.

Text copyright: Mark NeCamp, Jr. 2023

ISBN: 978 1 80341 454 6
978 1 80341 455 3 (ebook)
Library of Congress Control Number: 2023930438

A CIP catalogue record for this book is available from the British Library.

Design: Lapiz Digital Services

UK: Printed and bound by CPI Group (UK) Ltd, Croydon, CR0 4YY
Printed in North America by CPI GPS partners

We operate a distinctive and ethical publishing philosophy in
all areas of our business, from our global network of authors to
production and worldwide distribution.

Contents

I dedicate this work to my ancestors, gods, and teachers without whom this work would not exist; as well as the long line of practitioners- living and dead- that have done the never ending work of bearing and passing on the Promethean fire of Knowledge, Enlightenment, Reason, and Magick.

I also dedicate this to my friends, students, clients, and magickal colleagues that have been with me on the journey of life and the pursuit of wisdom and happiness.

Introduction

What is in these pages is magick. You can be balancing your chakras, doing hands on healing, casting a spell of protection, or casting a love spell and still be practicing a form of magick.

There are many definitions of magick. To me, magick is a calling; it is the soul's calling for the twin needs of safety and freedom, and the desire to make one's will real. It is both a means to an end, and a way of life. You can use all sorts of tools and techniques to do magick – and there are almost countless books, videos, and lectures on the subject – but what really makes someone a practitioner of the Art is to do magick and embrace all the wonder the World has to offer. The work before you covers the energy of magick itself in its most pure form.

Why We Do It

Magick can be done for many types of purposes such as healing, protection, financial gain, romantic love, and many others. Often, when someone wants to do magick, it is to benefit someone or something in ways they could not accomplish with normal, mundane means.

Magick is also a way to connect to others, the gods, the ancestors, and to the Universe itself. It is these connections that foster our spiritual development and can help us to become more than what we are.

What Is Energy Magick?

Energy magick is a way of practicing magick by directly manipulating reality. The aim of this book is to work directly with the sources of magickal and psychic energy with our hands, minds, and will to affect reality directly. You will not find traditional spellwork here. Your body will be the medium that magick happens and flows through. For example, instead of doing a healing ritual, one would work directly with the energies of healing and direct them to where they are needed.

When metaphysical techniques are first created, they come from mystical experiences. These experiences can come from anything from meditation to the use of psychedelics, or any prolonged stress on the body that liberates the body from its normal sensations and allows the consciousness to access a more subtle spiritual reality. In these mystical states, the practitioner discovers how to connect to the spiritual, manipulate and direct its energies, and affect changes in the physical world. Mysticism and magick are two sides of the same coin.

For example, a practitioner might fast and meditate for days to get into a trance state and they may have visions that they later record, sometimes using symbols and metaphor, in order to communicate the feelings and spiritual insights that they had. They can then use what they recorded and learned for future magickal workings. Another example is that a practitioner may dance intensely until they get into a trance state and then make certain movements with their body and feel inspired to feel certain emotions. These movements can be repeated to access those feelings later and be used as a tool for other workings.

The main differences between this book and most other books of magick are that:

1. It takes its foundation from the root practices and magickal philosophies of many common magickal schools and not just one.
2. This book uses virtually no physical tools.

This book is brought about from studying everything from New Age healing to Western Ceremonial Magick; Tibetan magick to Mexican Folk Sorcery. These are just examples and not the full list of sources. Magick is a common practice across history and the world. In the modern time, we must take a multi-faceted and cross-cultural approach. As someone that is multi-racial and has worked with teachers indigenous to the paths I mention, I am very sensitive to cultural appropriation and do my best not to cross that line. I honor the ancestors that have brought me to this place, the spirits of the land, and all physical and spiritual allies that have brought me here. What all these cultures have in common is that mystics brought down their insights and spiritual experiences into forms they could use later and pass on. I believe magick is for all, and at the same time we need to respect its roots.

If there are any tools used in this book, they will be mostly things you have around the home or are cheap to purchase. This has come about partially due to my practice, but also because I believe magick is ultimately a tool for our personal freedom and should not be restricted by economical means. Energy work is about what you can move and change and not the stuff you accumulate.

This is a book for both the novice and advanced practitioner. When I teach workshops, I often joke that I put the "work" in the workshop and this book is no different. The exercises are very direct and to the point because I do not want you to spend all your time reading about magick but not doing it. All the exercises can be done alone, but some can be done with a partner. If you find a subject that you already feel competent in in the beginning, please skip ahead; however, I may reference beginner exercises that relate to advanced ones.

I also want to make this book fun. There will be lectures, but also stories from my personal experience, case studies, and plenty of exercises to gain familiarity with the concepts.

I am going to assume that you have some familiarity in some standard "witchy" stuff like tarot (I draw on imagery from the *Rider-Waite-Smith* deck), crystals, magickal tools, etc. If something is not familiar, please take the time to look it up.

This book is divided into three parts:

- "Part I – Basic Energy Work" is a solid introduction to subjects such as basic energy work and meditation.
- "Part II – Advanced Energy Work" covers subjects such as banishing entities, consecrating a space, and moves onto invocation (the magickal art of drawing energies or external spirits through and inside you) and trance journeys through spirit realms.
- "Part III – The Energy Magick Grimoire" is where your mastery of the first sets of tools combines. This covers everything from spellwork to ritual. By weaving various techniques together, they become more complex, stronger, and more effective.

If you are an advanced practitioner that might want to skim the basics to get to the more "fun stuff" of Part II, I would humbly ask that you please read the summary at the beginning of each section to make sure that we are on the same page. At the very least the summary serves as a refresher of what basics are necessary. For the beginner, the summary serves to see exactly what we are about to get into.

I hope you enjoy working through the book and learning as I did when learning these techniques from various teachers and experiences over the years, and I wish you nothing but the best.

Note on Writing Style

I wrote this book as if I was having a conversation with you for the most part. I have been teaching at many festivals, occult stores, etc. for several years, and I try to take a conversational tone with you, the reader. On occasion, I will add some anecdotes. Also, I use magick with a "k" to differentiate it from stage magic, illusions, and things of that nature. Lastly, I often invite people to "see" and "feel" energy throughout this work. I acknowledge that many other psychic senses develop (such as "hearing" energy), or you may have other sensory issues (such as synesthesia), and where you find appropriate to your individual situation please feel free to adapt the exercises to your needs.

Part I
Basic Energy Work

Chapter 1

Grounding, Centering and Cycling

Summary: Energy, Grounding, Connecting with the Earth and Sky, Centering, Cycling, Cycling Living Energies, Cycling Other Energies

The ability for the sorcerer, witch, yogi, or general metaphysical practitioner to do anything effectively comes from their imagination, daring to dream, focus on a specific outcome, and allowing their intent to work through them to manifest their goals. The medium through which this all occurs is through energy. Energy, chi, prana – whatever you want to call it – is an invisible force that flows through all things. Magick is Change, and the constant flow of energy in the Universe speaks to that truth.

The course of this work is how to do magick through manipulating energy effectively. This mastery must be both internal and external, as they are both reflections of each other. This synergy between the internal and external worlds creates a harmony that not only fosters a sense of personal peace, but also makes magickal workings far more effective.

I used to be a far angrier and chaotic person before I started my journey into witchcraft, magick, and the occult. I have been able to find balance, some semblance of peace, and have learned how to grow. I am a better person than I used to be (even from yesterday), and I must give credit to both magick itself and the people that I have met on my spiritual journey.

I think tools in magick are fun to have, and I still have many of the tools I acquired when I first started out. I used a wand to direct energy, an athame to cast circles, a chalice to aid in purification, and a pentacle to help me bless my offerings among many others. I think what led me to using energy more directly was my training in energy healing that happened at the same time as my magickal instruction. I kept thinking to myself "Why should I use a wand when I can manipulate energy directly?" It was that question and a love of experimentation that led to some of the techniques and exercises below.

Energy

Energy – also called chi, prana, or psychic energy – is all around us. It is in our bodies, our food, our breath, the air, and everywhere else. This energy is connected to our emotions and shaped by our thoughts. I have found that energy follows some basic guidelines:

Energy is in everything. Everything is connected through energy, and it is everywhere. This means that potentially anything can be affected by the sorcerer, and the practitioner can be affected by anything.

Energy follows attention. Where you focus your awareness is where you will feel energy. It flows based upon where our attention goes. For example, when someone speaks to you and you listen, you are giving them energy.

Energy can be transformed. Energy can neither be created nor destroyed. It can only be transformed. Energy is in a constant state of flux and can be transformed by active or passive means. The sorcerer gains power from active harnessing and manipulating energy.

Energy can be changed based on intent and emotion. Active energy manipulation occurs from having the vision to see an outcome and transform that energy based upon that intention. Energy transformations can be sudden, but the more focus and care that is used, the better the outcomes.

Being aware of energy is the core of magick that works. My favorite exercise to start out with not only helps to gain confidence in the fact that everyone can do magick through moving energy but shows that you can feel magick directly without tools. This exercise offers direct proof that there is something bigger than us in a direct and quick manner. This is the first exercise my teachers taught me.

Exercise #1: Energy Ball
1. Breathe in and out. Imagine that as you breathe in and out, the invisible vital energy from around you is filling you.
2. Rub your hands together vigorously. Imagine that an invisible energy that you have gathered, is coming together where you rub your hands.
3. Keep rubbing your hands together.
4. Stop rubbing your hands, and then move them about an inch apart.
5. Move your hands closer to about a quarter inch apart, and then back to an inch a part.
6. Do this several times. You will feel warmth or a pressure. This is energy.
7. Repeat steps 1 through 5, but this time cup your hands together to make a ball made from that sensation of warmth of pressure.
8. Repeat steps 1 through 6, but make the ball larger and smaller. See what happens if you try to change how the ball feels. Play with different sensations.
9. When done, gently reabsorb your energy ball into your body. You can do this by thinking of your hand sucking it in, or even breathing it in. Play with different methods of doing this.

In the above exercise, you are dealing directly with the energy that is all around us, within you, and surrounding you. Do the exercise until it becomes very easy to make a ball. If you are having problems try the next exercise, "Grounding", since stress and doubt will often be blockages to getting in the right mindset to interact with energy in this way. If you at any time lose self-confidence in your craft, coming back to the simple energy ball can feel like a healthy way to recalibrate. Some schools will have you meditate before trying to move energy, and if you are having problems feeling energy, I highly recommend it. For me, I find that the more I have worked with energy, the faster I go into the relaxed state of meditation that effective magick requires. You can do magick angry – gods know I have blared Goth-industrial music while doing spells – and I have found it more useful to come from at least a neutral, relaxed place. That way you can clearly direct energy how you want it.

With practice, you should not have to rub your hands together to summon energy, you will be able to just do it, but if you have problems go back to the old method. I also find it helpful to rub my hands together to get started on energy work in order to re-sensitize my hands and get into a magickal mindset.

You may feel "buzzed" by playing with energy. By gathering, moving, and transforming energy our own personal life force can be affected. One of the essential skills of the practitioner is to ground this energy to the Earth.

Grounding

The goal of grounding is to connect to the Earth and in that connection find a neutral or energizing balance from which to do magick. As such, it is an essential exercise and a foundational skill to master. Grounding is simple in concept. The idea is that the Earth, by virtue of our connection to it, allows us to get rid of any unwanted energies, or simply ground them out in the way that an electrical ground protects electrical devices. Trees are experts at this, and in fact if you embrace a tree for a few minutes, you will feel the effect. The following exercise is a simple grounding exercise.

Exercise #2: Grounding

1. Sit, lie down, or stand. Close your eyes if you need to.
2. Take deep breaths and feel the weight of your feet. Try to feel the inside of your bones.
3. Think about how heavy your feet are.
4. Feel the weight of your legs and knees, as well as your feet.
5. Bring your awareness to the weight of all your lower body at once.
6. Continue this sense of awareness through your entire body – adding different body parts bit by bit until you are aware of the weight of your entire body from your head to your feet.
7. Imagine all the weight of your body bringing you closer to the Earth. Imagine that you are magnetized to the Earth.
8. Imagine and feel all the tension in your body, starting at your head and going to your feet, flows from your body to the Earth and through it to the Earth's core.
9. Breathe in and out, being aware of your body's connection to the Earth. Open your eyes if they are closed.

This is probably the simplest way to ground other than hugging a tree (who is arguably the greatest master of grounding). This should be mastered and practiced so that you can ground on command at any given moment. Mystical and spiritual experiences happen in the body as much as the spirit and connecting with the Earth and your physical body is prerequisite to much work. It is also a safety exercise for when we experience things that are overwhelming or just feel too much to handle. By being an expert in grounding, you can ground out negative energies directly and quickly. For example, let us say you are feeling a lot of negative energy after visiting a strange place. It would be in your best interest to ground out that energy if it affects you.

We can also ground in many ways other than meditation. Some people use dense stones such as hematite, take relaxing teas, or take ritual baths, but the focus here is to use as few tools as possible and work with the energy directly. What if you lose your favorite grounding stone? What if you can't take the time for a sacred bath? The Earth is easily accessible at any moment. You can be trying to relax before bed, in an office meeting, or doing anything else practically. Energy is always there for you.

Connecting with the Earth and Sky

To do magick effectively, most people need to start in a neutral, relaxed state as stated. This can be very challenging when we live in a world that is constantly demanding our attention. Our mental, physical, emotional, and spiritual energy are hijacked for various tasks that we must complete as part of our day-to-day life resulting in increased tension and stress. Magick comes from you, and if you want to do anything, from manifesting the love of your life to acquiring hidden knowledge, the magickal practitioner needs to be able to put the mundane world aside and focus on their craft. The easiest way to unplug from what is draining us and tap into something that will restore us is to connect to the most plentiful source of energy – the Earth and Sky.

Connecting to the Earth and Sky does the necessary step of bringing the practitioner to a magickal, neutral state and serves as a crucial source to limitless energy that does not drain, damage, or degrade them.

We are always influenced by the Earth. Our bodies are attuned to her magnetic energies that arise. We gain all our foodstuffs and material resources from her, and our bodies will eventually break down into her as well. To connect to Earth, is to really connect to the source of all we are materially, our place in the world, and to our essential nature as part of the cycle of life and death.

We are equally connected to the Sky, or Heavens. The moon and other planetary bodies affect us in subtle, but potent ways. We are connected energetically to the heavens and all that is above us. The Heavens are also the un-manifested Universe, pure Spirit, the potential for all things – where we are most connected to the Universe in its most raw state.

The Earth and Sky also have a philosophical meaning that underpins all energy work and magick, especially in the West. A sorcerer cannot manipulate the world unless they understand how to manipulate themselves. There is a saying from Hermetic magickal philosophy – "as above, so below". This typically means that the spiritual and the earthly worlds are mirrors of each other. It also means that humans are the intermediary between the Earth and the Heavens. Humans are collectively alchemists by nature, in that we are not only between these two forces, but we are the agents that can transform the energies of one to another. This is true in both Eastern and Western alchemy and magickal teachings.

It is important to note that energy is always flowing between Earth and Sky. The current that runs from Sky to Earth is typically the energy of manifestation and becoming. The energy that flows from Earth to Sky is typically of liberation, freedom, and release.

The next exercise builds off the first, and its goal is to not only ground energy to the Earth, but to cycle it back and forth between you and the Earth and the Sky. I mention energy in the last sentence, by this I mean the spiritual energy that is found within us and around us in all things. It is the binding force between all things, the medium in which magick happens, and what allows us to affect reality with magick. The next chapter will go into energy specifically, but for now we are dealing with the energy that resides within our bodies and the planet we are a part of. We are being that balancing point between Earth and Heaven, and harmonizing ourselves with them, and taking advantage of this connection to replenish ourselves.

Exercise #3: Connecting with Earth and Sky

1. Sit, stand, or lie down comfortably. Breathe as deeply and as slowly as you are able.
2. Imagine and feel the energy above your head and feel it slowly descend through your head and neck.
3. Imagine and feel energy moving further down past your head and neck, through your torso, your waist, your legs and down through your feet.
4. When you are at your feet, imagine the energy moving past your feet, past the ground, and through the Earth.
5. Imagine and feel the energy going further until it goes to the core of the Earth.
6. Breathe deeply, feel the connection to the Earth, and feel gravity comfortably bringing the energy of your body to the core. Rest comfortably in that connection for some time.
7. Still breathing deeply, imagine the energy coming from the core of the Earth, traveling upward, through the ground, and back through your body – all the way to the crown of your head and past it to the Sky. Rest comfortably in that connection.
8. When you breathe in – feel your connection from the core of the Earth and through your body to the Sky. Breathing out – feel the energy from the Sky, move through your head, through the rest of your body, and back to the Earth.
9. Take time to let the energies soak through your body, rejuvenate you, and remove any negativity, stress, or tension.

10. When you are ready to finish, focus on your center. This is your center of gravity, your dan tien, or your core. It is sometimes located below your navel. Focus any excess energy in your center.
11. Breathe in and out normally. Open your eyes if they are closed and take a few moments to pause and feel in your body.

The above technique can be used as part of a regular meditation practice, or just when you need it. This exercise also leads us to an important practice that goes hand in hand with grounding: centering. Gravity is our friend and teacher here. Just as we felt the gravity and weight in our bodies as we relaxed and grounded, so too can we focus on our center of gravity and how we can be at a natural point of balance with the energies of everything around us. Centering is shifting the attention from what we were grounding, or connecting to, and focusing just on ourselves in a positive and healthy way.

Centering

Centering itself is focusing on your core as in the above exercise. This can be done alone and should be mastered to do as easily and quickly as possible. You do not have to do the above meditation every time you want to center your energies.

An important aspect of centering is not just a way to relax or end a grounding exercise! It allows for internal focus and integration. Everything needs a foundation, and the cornerstone of any magickal working is a centered practitioner acting as that foundation. Integration of energy is the key to help you grow as a magickal practitioner – it allows the energies that circulate to collect and be stored for further magickal use for the replenishment of the practitioner's energy, and as a step in internal alchemy that we will cover in the section on Energy Work.

There is an old saying "if you don't stand for something, you will fall for anything." Centering helps create an energetic place that you can "stand". All magick starts with you. You are an energetic being whose actions, magickal and otherwise, start with you and radiate outwards. Without a stable center, you and your magick cannot blossom.

To center, all you need to do is bring your attention to it and relax into it. It is that simple. Your center may change based upon your body type, how your metaphysical energy courses and processes through your body, or even your mood. For some this place is right below the navel, for others it may be a little higher. It is important to understand that your center can be in flux, but what makes it your center at this very moment is based upon where the sum of your energy collects and is stable.

When you are centered in martial arts, it is difficult to be moved physically. In the same manner, when you are mostly centered and try to center yourself daily, you are focusing and strengthening your personal energy to the point that it is more and more difficult for it to be influenced by outside forces. For example, I am an empath and I can feel other people's emotions fairly well (it is a blessing and curse). When I notice that I am feeling something for no reason, I pause to center so I can connect with my own core and investigate whether those emotions are really from me or are they from someone outside my personal energy.

Cycling

Most writings on centering and grounding end there and typically only refer to the relationship between the practitioner and the Earth. My training in energy healing has taught me that cycling your personal energy is just as important. When I first started working with energy, I was often tired. I would do healing work on people and just feel drained. When I learned to cycle my energy, that all changed. I found that if I cycled my energy, as in the last exercise, I had a limitless pool of energy to harness and channel for whatever I needed. This is not to say that my pool of energy is infinite. I am still limited by the energy and resources my physical body needs to sustain itself.

For me, cycling energy comes from my study of martial arts and energy healing, especially Reiki. I have found that it takes little to no formal training to cycle your energy and reap the benefits of it.

You already were cycling your energy with the Earth and Sky, but that is just one type of energy cycling. There are two types of energy cycling: open and closed. Open is where the channel is continuous and free between you and what you are cycling your energy with. In the above exercise the channel was open between the energies of the Earth and Heavens/Sky. It is helpful to get good at that, so you can cycle your energies while barely thinking about it so you can focus on the subject that you are putting your attention and energy on. Closed cycling is useful to help remove energy blockages, feel good, general health, and as a prerequisite to cycling other energies along with yours. The below exercise is a closed technique to improve energetic circulation.

When we cycle energy, we are merely paying attention to a dynamic process that is happening all the time. The only difference is that we do it consciously.

Exercise #4: Closed Cycling

1. Start with grounding, as in *Exercise #2*.
2. When grounded, and while relaxing as much as possible, be aware of the energy of your feet and what it feels inside them. Breathe in deeply, and let your attention flow from a place below your feet, to your feet themselves, to your legs, and to your center. Breathe out.

3. Breathe in again at the level of your center, and as you breathe deep, follow the energy to your heart. Breathe out.

4. Breathe in at your heart and exhale. While you are exhaling, focus on the energy of your head and a place above your head. Breathe in again.

5. Breathe out and feel the energy flow from your head to your heart. Breathe in at the heart.

6. Breathe out to your center, being careful to feel the energy in your breath and body.

7. Breathe in.

8. Breathe out to your feet. Breathe into your feet, exhale to your center.

9. Keep following the pattern of breathing into an energy center (feet, center, heart, and head) and breathing out to the next. Repeat until this becomes a continuous cycle.

10. When you feel you are done, please collect the energy to your center.

11. The more slowly you do this technique the more relaxed you are, and the more quickly you do it the more energized (which might be nice if you want an energetic alternative to caffeine). The eventual goal when you cycle your energy is to do this one breath. The path from the feet to the head should be an inhale, and from the head to the feet should be an exhale.

Experimentation – When you can touch on all the energy centers with one breath, experiment with taking it slow as possible, and then as quickly (ground if you need to). What changes do you note?

Cycling Living Energies

Energy is constantly flowing. All we are doing is tapping into and manipulating that flow. The flow already exists. Everything is connected. Everything. Energy is just one medium through which we can explore that connection.

Have you ever gone into a large space and your feelings changed? Have you ever walked into a room and felt a difference? Your energies are automatically cycling with your environment. It is as natural as breathing. We are energetic creatures that respond to the people and places around us, much like a fish is changed by the water it swims within. When I walk into a forest, I feel something greater than myself. I feel the multitude of interconnected life. I breathe a little deeper, feel a little more connected, and can revel in the sum of Life that is greater than who I am as a solitary human.

The next exercise speaks directly to how we are connected energetically with other living things. It is an open cycling exercise where you will connect with a plant. If you want to do this with a partner or group, you can have the plant in the middle and you, and others can arrange around it in a circle. Once again, this energetic interaction happens naturally, we are only feeling and working with it consciously very much in the same way that we breathe automatically but can take deliberate breaths.

I love working with the energy of plants whether I am in a forest to find a release, making absinthe from herbs, or working in the garden. In modern energy work, we can connect with those plant energies and direct them based upon the chi we harness from them, as you would harness the energy in the Earth, or based upon their specific properties.

In the next exercise, instead of connecting to the energies of the Earth and Sky and cycling them through you – you are replacing them with the energy of plants.

Exercise #5: Cycling with Plants

1. Ground and center on your core.
2. Pay attention to the plant in front of you while taking deep breaths. Look at how vibrant the plant is and focus all your attention on it.

3. Cycle your energy from the Earth, through you, to the Sky, and back (like in *Exercise #3*).

4. When your energy is cycling on one breath, on the next inhale – imagine you are inhaling the plants energies and cycle that energy up and through you so that you are breathing from the plant, through your body, and back.

5. Breathing in, feel the energy coming from the plant to you. As you breathe out, feel the energy move from you to the plant.

6. When you are ready, center, and acknowledge or thank the plant in your own way.

Experimentation – Try this with indoor versus outdoor plants. This exercise can be done with trees and forests. If you garden, try connecting with your plants as seeds before your garden. If you do this over time, what changes do you see between you and the plant, or your connection to that plant?

If you wanted to use this exercise for a specific intent, let's say "healing", for example. You could cycle your energy with a healing plant like Echinacea (which is common to help boost the immune system) if you wanted to get that energy for your own well-being or even direct to help others.

I am choosing plants here on purpose. Plants are natural at getting near limitless energy from the Earth and have plenty to ethically spare. Cycling energy from a living person or animal is, of course, very possible, but then we are moving towards a psychic vampirism (which between consenting adults is fine), but it too often abused. Cycling energy from a human can have consequences. The person taking the energy can be addicted to taking life force in this manner, or one or both people can develop obsessions from the intensity of working with life energy directly.

While there should be caution in connecting energies to other living things that are not plants, it can be useful in many situations. You may want to also co-mingle energies for the purpose of creating more intimate connections with a magickal or romantic partner. Some people even do this as a group to help foster a type of hive of group energy which is called a group egregore.

Cycling Other Energies

You have already tapped into your connection with another living thing's energy. The benefits of doing this are to draw upon greater energy for magickal workings, but also to express the inherent connection all things share.

This is where things get more interesting. Why stop with living things? Why not tap into the connection you have with the moon or sun? What about other planetary energies, such as the planets that are used in astrology? What about other cosmic phenomena?

The next exercises are to cycle your energy with the most common of heavenly bodies that we have an affect us on a regular basis: the sun and moon. If possible, do the next two exercises outside where you can see the sun or moon. If not, be aware of where the sun and moon are in relation to you while you are indoors. A practitioner must also master channeling energy they cannot directly see. For example, if I wanted to channel the planetary energies of Mercury for communication, I would probably not wait to take out a telescope and see the planet Mercury physically before I begin my work. In my opinion, a practitioner should not let any obstacle get in the way of the energy they are trying to channel and work with.

Cycling your energies directly with nature – whether it is the earth or any heavenly body, is a great way to connect to the Universe in its rawest form. This is where magickal techniques and spiritual evolution come together. We gain power through knowledge of our connection and evolve by living essential spiritual truths such as the fact that "everything is connected". We also gain power by knowing how to harness those energies. The next exercise is directly cycling your energy from a plentiful heavenly body: the sun.

Exercise #6: Cycling the Sun

1. Gain awareness of the sun by knowing its position in the sky (do not look directly at the sun).
2. Close your eyes.
3. Get into a relaxed state by grounding and then cycling your energy between the Earth and Sky/Heavens.
4. Envision the sun in your mind's eye. Imagine the solar energies descending upon you. When you are ready, breathe in, and consciously take in the energies of the sun by breathing it in when your "in" breath is at the top of your head.
5. Cycle the energies through your body, exhaling through your feet.
6. Inhale the energies of the sun again, make sure that you are going through the place above your head, to your head, your heart, your center, your feet, and below your feet.
7. Exhale and feel that connection to the sun.
8. Repeat this cycling for a few minutes.
9. Inhale the energies and exhale while feeling that connection until you feel you are full of the energies of the sun.
10. Pause to rest with the energies of the sun inside you and absorb them into your center.
11. Ground any excess energy only if you wish. Open your eyes if they are closed.
12. For energies from the Heavens, it is more effective if you breathe them in from the energy source to your head,

through your body and back. For terrestrial energies, such as the Earth – it is typically easier to breathe in through the feet. Feel free to experiment and find what works best for you.

The next exercise can be done inside or outside. Instead of just cycling the energy of a heavenly body, you will harness and hold it. If you need to, please re-familiarize yourself with making energy balls. Next, we are going to connect and harness the energies of the moon. Before you do this exercise, research where the moon is in the sky in relation to you and its specific phase.

Exercise #7: Harnessing the Moon

1. Ground.
2. Gain awareness of the moon by looking at it directly or knowing its position.
3. Close your eyes.
4. Cycle your energy between the Earth and Sky/Heavens.
5. Look at or envision the moon. See and feel the lunar energies descending over and through you.
6. Consciously take in the energies of the sun by breathing them into you directly. Exhale and feel that connection.
7. Inhale the energies and exhale while feeling that connection until you feel you are full of the energies of the moon.
8. Hold out your hands and make an energy ball, but instead of using your own energy – use the energy of the Moon.
9. Hold that lunar energy in your hands. As you breathe in, feel that ball getting more and more intense.
10. Release the energy back to the moon, by imagining it going from your hands to the moon or absorb into your body by breathing it into your body.
11. Center. Open your eyes if they are closed.
12. Thank or acknowledge the Moon in any way you see fit.

The Moon is the heavenly body that connects us to many different things – especially feminine energy, emotions, and dreams. You can connect with those aspects and many more through this exercise. The Moon, and any heavenly body, has limitless energy to share.

Some people ask why you would cycle your energies with the moon at all. The Moon, aside from affecting the physical tides of the oceans, affects our subtle energies just as much. In energy work, it is often in our best interest to work with Nature and not against it. This doesn't mean that you must work with natural cycles all the time, but it means that everything has cycles and the changes of the external world affect the internal world. This is also true in the opposite – we affect the external world all the time by how we manage our internal energies and thoughts.

Experimentation – If you were doing this exercise in a group, you could pass around the energy ball you make and add to it before finally releasing it with a specific intention. Instead of absorbing the lunar energy into your body, release it into a beverage to bless and share or even into an object such as a crystal.

When working with energies that you cycle from terrestrial or celestial sources, remember to give thanks. Gratitude builds another type of energetic relationship with the natural forces we use and join ourselves with.

There are no limits in what you can connect your energy with and its effects. This is especially true when you work with metaphysical correspondences. For example, since Mercury is the planet of communication, you could cycle your energies with that planet to increase your personal ability to communicate with others.

Be very careful in cycling energies with another living person. Without permission, you run the risk of unethical psychic vampirism. Just as you would not touch someone physically without their permission, you would not do so energetically.

Another useful purpose of cycling is in working with deities. When we pray to the gods we connect with them. You can make your prayers have a further energetic component by cycling your energies with the gods. In practice, you can cycle with a statue of the deity or the point outside of yourself that you feel the deity emanates from. As you would with a person in the flesh, ask permission. You may have to give offerings that are appropriate to that deity. In this way, the energy of the gods is not something outside of ourselves, but something we can take within. Creating an energetic bridge with a deity usually happen naturally in giving offerings (where the energetic aspect of the offering goes to the deity), and through prayer and meditation, and cycling with purpose can give an extra potency to you work. I do caution that doing that does have the potential to take on traits of the deity or spirit, so please be careful what energies you connect with.

Remember we are connecting with the spiritual energy of the subject, not the physical. Everything has an energetic body. The next chapter deals with our internal energies, we as energetic beings, and the different metaphysical parts that something is composed of.

Chapter 2

Aura and Energetic Bodies

Summary: The Aura, Energetic Bodies, Basic Energy Healing, Shielding, Invisibility, The Seven Chakras, The Four Elemental Functions of the Chakra, "Lesser" Chakras

Just as the Earth and Heavens are reflections of each other, so too are the internal and external worlds mirrors of each other. As such, the body of the Universe can be understood and shaped in relation to how we understand and shape our own spiritual bodies. Therefore, knowledge of the self is necessary to manipulate the world around us.

Energy is constantly flowing between you and the various realms of existence, and between you and other living things. Our energetic bodies are dynamic creatures that are constantly in a state of flux. The aura, or auric body, is a manifestation of that constant movement and is typically a layer of energy that wraps around the physical one. The aura itself has at least two main layers: an inner layer being 1 to 2 finger widths from the skin, and at least one outer layer that can extend up to several feet from the first.

The Aura

The aura is somewhat of a protective barrier between you and your main energetic body, or energetic double, which occupies the same space your physical body does. It can be a variety of colors and textures and can vary in intensity based upon the energy level and mood of the person. Many books ascribe various colors to them, but I find that depends on how you program your mind to accept that information. While one person may see many colors, another may see none. For one person the colors can correspond to what they feel like are different corresponding moods (for example, red=anger), or even the seven major chakras.

The next exercises are to sense the energetic body that we all have. The more you sense energy, the easier it is to manipulate. These exercises can also be done in a group setting by having one person try to sense the aura and the other person being the one observed and then switching places. If you have problems feeling the aura, you can warm up your "hand chakras" by opening and closing your hands rapidly 10-15 times to open your psychic ability to feel.

Exercise #8: Sensing the Aura

1. Rub your hands together to get them sensitive to feeling energy.
2. Take time to feel both sides of your hand, starting at one side and then the other.
3. "Pat" your hands with energy by moving to touch your hand but stopping about ¼ to 1 inch, 1 to 3 centimeters, from touching.
4. Move your hands as far apart as possible, then move your hands closer together slowly – moving at 3 to 4 inch, or 7 to 10 centimeters, increments. Gradually feel for warmth or pressure.
5. Notice where you first feel pressure and any places that you do that are closer.
6. Repeat from the beginning but explore as much as your body as you can, so that you can feel your aura consistently.
7. Repeat this exercise by feeling your aura with your arm extended from as far back as you can reach; gradually move one hand closer to your other to feel the outer layer. It should extend some distance from the inner one.

8. Center when done exploring your inner and outer aura. If you feel strange afterwards, cycle your energy between Earth and Sky and ground.

Experimentation – If you have a partner, try feeling the aura from several feet away and gradually walk towards the other person's aura with hands extended to feel the outer aura. What does it feel like to walk into another person's aura consciously?

Since some people are oriented in one sense more than another, here is a way to sense the aura using "second sight". "Second sight" is the psychic ability to see things that are overlaid over the physical. This is different from traditional clairvoyance that is more about seeing psychic visions.

Exercise #9: Seeing the Energetic Body

This exercise is designed to focus your "second sight" and help you feel energy more directly. Some people "see" better than others and it may take time to develop. This is also known as the "body of light", "etheric double", or astral body.

1. Close your eyes.
2. Imagine that your body is made entirely of white light.
3. Open your eyes and then close them again. Go back to the visualization that you are made of white light.
4. Look in your mind's eye at the body of light. Look for any dark spots and make note of them.
5. Repeat as many times as necessary to make this body of light become sharper and clearer in your mind's eye.

Experimentation – Try doing this exercise in a dark room. Is it easier to see the body of light? Is this easier meditating, or grounding? Cycle your energy while doing this exercise. Are there any changes?

The above exercises are important to master since seeing and feeling energy is tied directly to the ability to change it. It is good to train both senses of "sight" and "touch", even if one is stronger than the other. Most of your energetic body should be bright, while the dark spots are any places that need healing. There is an intrinsic relationship between your energy and physical body. It is not uncommon to do energy healing to help the physical body and its processes. At the same time, the health of the physical body can determine the health of your energy. It is important to keep both your energetic and physical bodies in good order so that they can really function in a healthy synergy.

Energetic Bodies

The previous exercises helped get you in touch with the part of us that is composed of energy. Typically speaking as a magickal practitioner, when I talk of the body, I do not mean just the physical body. I am really talking about four distinct parts of the self. These four parts are the physical body, energetic (astral or emotional) body, mental body, and the soul. These go by slightly different names depending on the tradition and are outlined below.

Physical – This is the part of your body that feels physical sensation and houses your vital life force. It is this body that is born, changes and eventually dies.

Energetic/Astral – This is the part of your body that we are dealing with the most in this book. It is your emotional or astral body. This is the part of you associated with your feelings and intuitions. It is the body that can travel and is the most vulnerable to other people. In a very real way, we connect with other people through our emotions and your energetic body is not only within you but extends and radiates outside of you. The more we open to people, and they to us, the more we feel connected. Your energetic body has its own anatomy that is as complex as your physical. It includes your aura, the 7 major chakras (other schools of thought deal with many more); energetic channels connecting you to Earth and the realm of Spirit, and hundreds if not thousands of minor vortices of energy and lines that connect them. While your physical body decomposes easily when you die, your energetic body can stick around longer in some cases, but eventually can decompose, be destroyed, or sent on.

Mental Body – Thought shapes reality. Our thoughts are the wind that can move the tides of our emotions. Our mental body is mostly our thoughts and is also the intermediary force between our consciousness and our soul.

Soul – Some say the soul is the spark of the Divine, and as such we will associate it with Fire. If there was an event that created the Universe, then at one point all is One. The soul is that piece of the One. I am not venturing into a place of monotheism, but I am adhering to the mystical teaching that we have a common beginning and an intrinsic connection. Your soul is theoretically the part of you that goes from incarnation to incarnation, or to some other place. We will leave that mystery for others to ponder.

Basic Energy Healing

Healing is one of the basic purposes of magick – healing for the self or others. Before we go around healing people like some miracle worker, we need to focus on the self. Like the physical body, the energetic body can suffer normal wear and tear and as a result needs upkeep and maintenance on occasion.

The next exercise is a basic energy healing exercise. Practice this on yourself first since improper use of this exercise has the potential to harm another living thing by accident. I was doing healing work with a teacher on someone that had lung damage. I cleaned myself up energetically afterwards, but a strange thing happened. The next day I developed a bad cold that turned into bronchitis. I was sick for a couple of weeks. What I realized I did wrong was that I had taken in too much of that person's sick energy and used too much of my personal energy. I should have cycled my energy with the Earth and Heavens, and I should have taken proper precautions of energetically shielding and cycling my energy better.

Exercise #10: Basic Energy Healing (Self)
1. Ground and center.
2. Cycle your energy between Earth and the Heavens.
3. Visualize your body of white light. Look for any dark spots in the energetic body.
4. Imagine and feel any darkness filled in and restored with white light.
5. Repeat as necessary.
6. Ground and center to close.
7. You can heal the aura the same way, and I encourage you to do that, but your vision needs to expand outward from the outline of your physical body to your inner and outer aura.

Personal healing should happen on a regular basis, and it is good to check out your energy as part of your regular magickal practice. We will cover energy healing more in the chapter on advanced healing, since healing another person requires mastery of the basics. If you already feel like you have a good grasp on cycling, shielding, energy movement, and knowledge of energy bodies – feel free to skip ahead and explore that section.

Shielding

We have gone over what energy is and some basics for drawing it into our lives. It bears mentioning that not all energy is beneficial. Have you ever been in a room that didn't feel right or been to a place after people have argued? Even though most people are not magickal practitioners, almost everyone can affect energy. There are many times when you don't want to be exposed to, or be influenced by, the energy around you. Shielding can be done, when you feel uncomfortable or unsafe, before any magickal work, to create a safe bubble when you are upset, or anytime you need it. The next exercise is how to construct a basic, personal shield.

Exercise #11: Personal Shields

1. Ground and center.
2. Breathe slowly in and out. As you breathe slower and slower, imagine that you begin to feel safe or protected.
3. Imagine a color that makes you feel safe or protected. Imagine, see, and feel your aura and energy body filling up with that color.
4. Maintaining your breathing, and when you feel as safe or protected as you are able, think of a word that symbolizes what you are feeling right now. Say that word aloud.
5. Say the word at least two more times while you are feeling safe or protected and imagining your personal energy the specific color you visualized.
6. Ground and center to close.

All you must do to get to your personal shield is to think of that color and say that word. The use of keywords like this helps to build your toolbox of magickal techniques that can be accessed quickly and built upon.

Shielding is necessary in healing others so that you maintain an energetically sterile environment, just like when a doctor puts on a mask, gloves, and scrubs. It is a crucial and useful tool when exploring both physical and metaphysical places – such as going on an astral journey to a place you have never been before.

Experimentation – If you are working with a partner, try this exercise with one person feeling the outer edge of your aura and have them note any changes.

Shaping and influencing energy is crucial to creating practical effects. In the personal shielding exercise, you learned how to manipulate your own energy with your imagination. I have found shielding to be one of the most useful tools for the magickal practitioner. I can shield energy that is negative, whether it comes from a person or place, and protect myself when I need to. If you have toxic family members, this might be the one technique that makes family gatherings tolerable! Before any major magick, most people will purify themselves and their space, but neglect to shield. It is not that you need to spend the rest of your life in a bubble; you are really using your aura as a tool and having a healthy boundary.

Boundaries are necessary in magick. Sometimes we blur those lines on purpose, such as using the psychic skill of empathy consciously, but we all need to learn to come back to who we are. In this way, shielding and centering go hand in hand.

The shield can have any property. You can repeat the shielding exercise to create an arsenal of different shields. Here are a few useful ones with examples of colors and properties. The below are just suggestions. You can use any color, property, and word together. These are just ones that I have used and seem to make sense for other people.

Shield Type	Purpose	Key Word	Color
Protection	Strong, solid protection from all energies	no	Black
Filter	Screening out negative energies and letting in positive ones	Screen	Gray
Peace	To foster a sense of peace when the world is too chaotic or painful	peace	Blue
Aggressive	Proactive shield to ward people off	go	Red
Grounding	Used to ground out any energies the shield reacts to	ground	Earth tones

I remember hanging out late at night with a buddy of mine and we found ourselves walking alone down a dark street. My friend was very inebriated (luckily, I was sober) and I had his arm over my shoulders – propping him up to help him walk. After a while, I could see two people coming towards us, and oddly enough it was two guys with one guy propping his friend up like I was. They pass by us, and my buddy brushes up against them. Suddenly the two guys think we want a fight. Since I was basically one armed at this point – with my arm around my friend – I really didn't want to get into a fight. I made my aura as dark as possible – deeply black and threatening – and hissed at them. The two antagonists screamed, "They're vampires!" and quickly ran down the street out of our sight. Energy work does have practical applications.

Note for Empaths

Many magickal practitioners can use empathy, the psychic skill of feeling and projecting emotions. I have found that shielding helps harness and practice this skill effectively. Empathy works both ways – receptive and projective – with receptive being used most. I used to be overwhelmed by empathy. I would often feel other people's emotions before my own and get very overwhelmed by them.

After some training in shielding, I was able to get a handle on things. For me, it was not about having a solid energetic shield or armor all the time, it was about using the "screen" ability of a shield to filter out other people's emotions and feel mine and another's at the same time and have healthy boundaries between the two. I encourage all empaths reading this to do the following:

1. Learn to shield and filter out energy.
2. Ground out emotions that are too much.
3. Center to feel your emotions versus another person's feelings.

For projective empathy, you can change your shield to any emotion and project it outwards. To cheer up someone, you can brighten your shield, meditate on a color like yellow, and project it outwards. Really, projective empathy is what we are doing when we are doing any type of aggressive shield. Empathy is a two-sided coin.

Invisibility

Sometimes you may not want to shield directly. Shielding does imply that you are shielding from something that you are in some sort of conflict. Perhaps, you wish to escape the energetic conflict that is occurring or even avoid it altogether.

People, even non magickal people, sense each other through many ways – especially the aura. When someone with a "high energy" aura comes into the room, we notice almost immediately, but we may not notice a person with a "low energy" aura right away. The goal of the next exercise is to mimic someone with low energy by compressing our aura as tight as we can and at the same time change our energy to mirror that of the energy to that of our surroundings as a sort of camouflage.

Exercise #12: Invisibility

1. Center.
2. Be aware of the edges of your aura and your astral body.
3. Bring the outer edge of your aura to your inner edge by willing it to do so. See, feel, and imagine this happening slowly.
4. Be aware of your breathing. As you breathe in and out, imagine that your combined aura is made of a mirror.
5. Imagine the energy of your surroundings sliding off the smooth surface of your mirrored aura and reflecting any excess energy that touch your aura.
6. Keep imagining the sliding and reflective surface of your aura as much as you can.
7. If you need to, think of a key word that stands for this state of being.
8. When you are done, imagine your aura going back to a neutral state.
9. Visualize and feel your outer aura returning to its proper place.
10. Ground and center.

The more you feel your aura, the easier it is to manipulate. Learning to manipulate the aura and your energetic body is another key skill of the sorcerer, but knowledge is power. Knowing as much about the energetic body as possible is needed so that you know what you must work with and what you can in fact manipulate. Energy is shaped by intention, but we all need to know what that is before we can change it.

The energetic body has its own anatomy, just like the physical body. One of the most well-known parts of the energetic body is the "7 chakras". Most people say 7, but there are rather more than that. For now, we are going to explore the chakras and the major centers of the energetic body. While chakras come from the spiritual culture and teachings of India, there are other systems of chakras that are just as valid such as the "Three Celtic Cauldrons" which focus on the head, heart, and belly.

The Seven Chakras

The chakras have been popularized through other practitioners and the emergence in popularity of yoga. Each chakra or "wheel" of energy is a specific center in the body and is attributed to its own color scheme. The reason each chakra is different is because we are natural prisms for the energies that flow through us from Heaven to Earth and back again. The chakras are a spectrum of consciousness from the material to the undifferentiated spiritual – they are a byproduct of the natural cycling of energy through our bodies as revealed through our astral bodies.

Chakras function as "centers" of energy as it is transformed from Earth to Sky and through your energetic body, but also as repositories for that energy to collect. As such, chakras are like organs of your astral body. All seven chakras are connected by one long column called the sushumna and are powered by the currents that connect Heaven and Earth continuously called Ida and Pingala.

They can be damaged by life and trauma just like your aura and main energetic double and should be maintained on a regular basis. Chakras can be worn, torn, blocked (as in the flow of energy is blocked), depleted, or even have an excess of energy.

Most people focus on the seven chakras since they are easy to grasp and focus on major energy centers. There are many books on chakras, so if you want to read further on that subject there are a multitude of sources to choose from, but I will give a simple overview as it pertains to our work. Here is an easy reference list:

Chakra Location	No.	Consciousness	Color
Root / Base of Spine	1st	Physical World Physical Needs	Red
Sacral / Below Navel	2nd		Orange
Solar Plexus	3rd	Will	Yellow
Heart	4th	Love	Green Pink
Throat	5th	Communications	Blue
Third Eye	6th	Insight Imagination	Violet
Crown	7th	Divine Connections Higher Self	Indigo White

Each chakra governs a different mode of consciousness and corresponding aspect of life. There is a two-way relationship between your chakra's health and the healthy ability to function in the corresponding sphere of someone's life. For example, someone that has problems talking about and processing emotions may have a weak, or blocked, sacral chakra. A person that works too much may have an overabundance of energy in their 3rd chakra. Damage to the Third Eye may inhibit someone's imagination.

On the other side of this, healing a chakra can help a person with that corresponding mode of life. It is worth taking note about how energy affects the greater world. Energy is subtle. Doing a healing on someone's chakra is not often a "cure all", but it can assist a person in making the corresponding changes in their life. From the example above of a person that works too much – healing their 3rd chakra won't stop them from over working, but by feeling the differences in their body they will know what health feels like and can be empowered to make different choices. In that same example, if the person that was addicted to work was able to work more reasonably, their 3rd chakra would probably come back to a reasonable condition.

I have seen some amazing changes due to energy healing of the chakras. A client of mine that was emotionally blocked was able to release long repressed energies due to the chakra healing I performed and was able to start a healing journey that changed her life drastically. For my own personal work, doing work on my heart chakra to heal trauma has helped me see more love in the world and more importantly helped me love myself.

Just like with the body of light, we cannot heal until we diagnose the problems. There are three main ways to diagnose chakra problems: seeing them in "second sight", feeling the energy directly, or using a tool such as a pendulum. For my own chakras, I typically will feel the energy and use sight; with other people I will use sight with a pendulum since it is less intrusive. In the spirit of this work, where we want to not be reliant on tools – below is an exercise to explore our chakras.

This exercise uses our sight in conjunction with our ability to feel energy. Before you begin the exercise, sit, or lay down comfortably. Also, it helps a lot to re-sensitize your hands to energy by doing the energy ball exercise, rub your hand together for some time, or open and close your hands – alternating between outstretched fingers to making a fist, very quickly at least 10 times. When you are feeling the energy of the chakra, feel for energy that is hovering just over your physical body. It will feel different from the inner layer of your aura. While doing this exercise you can pause between each chakra to take notes if you wish, so please keep something to make notes with nearby. Lastly, before you start familiarizing yourself with the above chart. If you need to you can take breaks between each chakra to look at the chart for reference if needed.

Exercise #13: Chakra Self-Check

1. Close your eyes and breathe until you are taking slow, deep breaths.
2. See and feel your body of energy.
3. Pay attention to the area at the base of your spine. See and feel internally an area that looks red. Take note of any emotions, feelings, and sensations. The more you focus on that area, the more apparent the energy will be.
4. Use one or both of your hands to feel the energy above the area. Feel the outline of the chakra. Does it feel warm or cool? Intense or weak?
5. Breathing in and out, move your awareness to the next chakra. You are looking for an energy that looks orange near the navel. See and feel the energy. Explore it with second sight and touching the energy.
6. Repeat for each chakra. Look for energy based upon the color and area of each chakra.
7. Pause to take notes or study the chart if needed. If you pause, take a few deep breaths to get back into a relaxed state of mind.
8. After exploring the crown chakra, ground, and center.
9. If you have a friend to help you, you can have them take notes on your observation of each chakra and compare your individual findings. The next exercise is to help maintain chakra health and healing. This can be repeated for all the chakras.

Exercise #14: Opening Chakras

1. Ground and center.
2. Cycle your energy, but this time cycle through each chakra – feeling each center and seeing them in your mind's eye. Cycle the energy from the Earth to each of the seven major chakras, to the Heavens, and back.

3. Cycle and pause your energy at the relevant chakra. Imagine and feel the chakra as a point of light in your body.
4. See and feel that point of light becoming larger, warmer, and more intense. See the colors get more vibrant in your inner sight and feel the warmth of the chakra as much as you are able.
5. Breathe in energy into your chakra and imagine it moving and circulating.
6. Hold your breath momentarily and feel the energy become more solid and dense in the chakra.
7. Exhale and breathe out through that chakra.
8. Hold the exhale as much as possible and inhale again repeating Steps 5 and 6. Do this several times.
9. Move onto another chakra if you wish.
10. Ground and center.

You can start the above exercise at the root and go all the way to the crown or do one chakra at a time. Some people open and "close" their chakras in the same exercise. I prefer not to "close" them since the above exercise should regulate the energy in a healthy way. This exercise was also done with the purpose of using the four-fold function of each chakra.

The Four Elemental Functions of the Chakra

Some books on the chakras try to equate the four elements with the seven chakras somehow. I have found it more advantageous to think that the energy of the four elements is expressed in terms of how the chakras function. The energy of the chakras is not only around us in Nature, but within ourselves. The following is how the elements relate to the chakras' functions:

Water – When we breathe in the chakras, we are receptive to that chakra energy like water. We drink in energy to nourish ourselves and quench our need for that energy.

Fire – When we circulate that energy, it moves like energetic fire through the chakra. It burns away any impurities and speaks to the dynamic nature of flow of energy.

Earth – When we hold that energy in for ourselves, it is held like earth. Chakras have a place in the physical body, and as much energy flows in and out of each chakra some energy remains to maintain who we are and reflects our consciousness.

Air – When we express that chakra energy, we are using its air function. Air in many metaphysical systems refers to creativity. The ability to express each chakra in our behaviors in the world creatively speaks to this.

Once again, there is a symbiotic relationship between the chakra and the mode of existence and consciousness they oversee or influence. Below is a list with further correspondences.

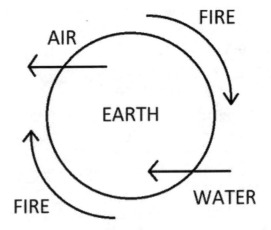

Chakra	Color	Key Word	Life Area
Root	Red	Survival	Money Bills Food
Sacral	Orange	Pleasure	Sex Friendship Social Relationships
Solar Plexus	Yellow	Will	Work Partnership Responsibilities
Heart	Green	Love	Love Betrayal Hate
Throat//Hobbies	Blue	Expression	Projects Likes & Dislikes Hobbies
Third Eye	Violet	Vision	Imagination Outlook Psychic Ability
Crown	Indigo	White	Union Religion Spirituality

"Lesser" Chakras

I would also like to add the following "lesser chakras" since we use them on a regular basis. There are literally hundreds of chakras, and these can be seen in everything from reflexology to Chinese acupuncture to yoga asanas. While these chakras do not traditionally have colors associated with them, I have found it useful to just see them as points of light.

Chakra Location	Function
Feet	Expressing energy to the world
Hands	Receiving and manipulating energy
Above Head	Connect to the Heavens
Below Feet	Connect to the Earth

Experimentation – Try *Exercise #14* above with the lesser chakras. Make notice of what you perceive.

The chakras are not the only part of your energetic body, but they are a large component. By now, your toolbox of knowledge of the energetic body includes the body as an energetic double of white light that has energy centers known as chakras – both major and minor. The next section is about the manipulation of energy as it pertains to the self, but more so how you can personally control it.

Chapter 3

Fundamentals of Energy Work

Summary: Manipulating Energy, Five Elements, Sending and Receiving Energy, Purification, Enchantment, Energetic Alchemy (Four Step Process)

I was doing healing work on someone in the southwest of America. They had been feeling unwell for some time and felt they were under attack by a sorcerer. I put up a shield but had the shield close to my skin as much as possible – like an energetic set of clothes. I had them lie down and rest while I inspected their aura and energetic field. I was able to find a piece of energy lodged in their body that was the shape of a dart. When I touched it, they cried out in pain. I removed the dart and grounded the energy. The client started to feel much better.

By this time, you have made a few energy balls. Now it is time to practice some more advanced techniques. The next exercise is to master shaping the energy of the ball. It is a small and harmless bit of energy that you have raised for your personal use.

Please keep in mind that while we are playing around for fun at this point, energy can be very serious. If you were doing the self-healing exercise above, you could do harm if you decided to fill in the white light with darkness. In this way, you could cause serious damage to yourself.

Manipulating Energy

At this point, you are familiar with the energy of the self. Now we can deal with how you handle energy that enters your personal sphere. The manipulation of energy is simple in theory but takes practice and experience to master. The next exercise is to further explore and play with energy to get on the road to mastery. I do not use the word "play" lightly. The goal of magick is not just to get what you want, but to evolve and grow. Modern psychology speaks much of the "child" self – the part of us that is creative and wants to use play as a tool to grow, learn, and explore. We cannot get out of the boredom of our stagnancies unless we are willing to look at the world with wonder. In this sense "play" is our Divine right and we are justified to play to become more than what we are.

Exercise #15: Energy Ball 2

1. Ground and center. Cycle your energy between Earth and Sky.
2. Create an energy ball.
3. Make your energy ball as big as a bowling ball, or larger.
4. Hold the ball in one hand and pet it with the other.
5. Hold the ball upside down and be aware of its weight and how it feels.
6. Hold the ball right side up and close your eyes. Look at the ball with "second sight" and see it as a ball of white light.
7. Change the color of the ball to anything you want, then back to white.
8. Absorb the ball with your hands. You can also breathe it in if you wish.
9. Be aware of your breathing. Cycle your energy openly with the Earth and Sky if you feel drained.
10. Make a large energy ball, and then close your hands together closer and closer to make a small, dense energy ball.
11. Change the temperature of it to as hot as possible – imagining that the ball is burning bright and hot in your hand.
12. Change the temperature of the ball back to room temperature, and then to as cold as possible. Change it back to room temperature after some time has passed.

13. Absorb the ball.
14. Make a new ball that is any size you wish. Hold it for a few moments. Imagine the ball has different textures – make it go from smooth (as if it was made of metal or glass) to something with texture (bumps, spikes, etc.). Hold the ball in one hand, while you explore the textures with another.
15. Absorb the ball.
16. Ground and center.

Energy can be shaped in almost any way. Now, it is time to move on from the "ball" to other shapes. So far, we have really worked with manipulating the quality of energy we already have. In this case, we have been using the chi of our bodies as supplied by our fundamental connection to Earth and Sky. That is not enough. We need to be able to change the fundamental property of the energies themselves.

Note About Egregores

You may have noticed that the energy felt different when you did different shapes. This is by virtue of the fact that "form follows function". While we can ascribe any correspondence to anything (for example, the color of mourning in the West is black, while in Asia it is often yellow) some things flow more naturally than others. I said some time ago that we need to work typically with Nature and not against it. While this is true, we also need to think about the egregore of that knowledge. An egregore is the sum of energy, experience, and usage that a thing possesses. The egregore of knowledge for the occult properties of fire, for example, typically are that of action, change, and transformation. It is easier for the sorcerer to work with some of these correspondences, and work with the body of lore and experience that is attached to it.

I am mentioning egregores, because not only is it an important magickal concept that gets overlooked, but the next section is regarding the elements – which is an important egregore set to work with.

Five Elements

Almost every magickal system has something to say about the elements – the metaphysical building blocks of the Universe. In the West, they are typically broken down into a system of four or five. The main four elements are usually Air, Fire, Water, and Earth with the fifth element being Spirit. The elements, like all energy, dwell within us and around us. The only major difference is that the elements are specialized forms of energy. Evoking the elements calls us to focus on their specific attributes – qualities that have been talked about and worked with since the time of the ancient Greeks. Think of the elements as different flavors of the energy we already work with. Below is a list regarding their elements and their correspondences.

Element	Attributes	Color(s)	Platonic Solid
Air	Thought/Mind Imagination Beginnings	Yellow	Octahedron (8 sides)
Fire	Movement Transformation Energy	Red	
Water	Emotions Purification Healing	Blue	Icosahedron (20 sides)*
Earth	The body Fertility Stability Money	Green	Cube/ Hexahedron (6 sides)
Spirit	Spirituality The Universe The Divine	Purple or None	Dodecahedron (12 sides)*

*To be perfectly honest, using a sphere for these shaped works almost as well, and is an acceptable substitute.

Most times when people talk about the elements it is also in relation to the four directions in the Western occult tradition (air-east, fire-south, water-west, earth-north), but I wanted to make an emphasis on shapes since we have been changing the physical shape of the energy. Changing the shape of energy not only changes its function, but also its fundamental nature to some degree. If I was doing healing work on someone and channeling energy from them the Universe to them, I might make a cone of energy to direct the healing to them. In this case, I altered the energy in terms of not only the type of energy, but how and why it moves.

In the chart and diagram above, I included shapes from the school of sacred geometry: the platonic solids. These were created by Plato and given elemental assignments over time. The next exercise is to channel energy shape and property. Now it is time to combine what we know about the elements and their shapes with our ability to manipulate energy.

Exercise #16: Energy Shapes

1. Study the section of the chart for Earth and Fire. If you need to, do meditation on each of the elements on your own.
2. Ground and center. Cycle your energy between Earth and Sky.
3. Create an energy ball.
4. Feel the energy. See the ball if you can, using "second sight".
5. Shape the ball into a cube. Imagine the smooth sides of the cube and feel its texture. Use your hands to shape the energy along with your imagination.
6. Use one hand to hold the cube while using the other to touch the individual exposed sides, while holding it with the other.
7. Make your cube as dense as possible.

8. Imagine that the cube is green and made of the earth. Think about all the attributes of earth energy in terms of nature and the physical world.

9. Take a few moments of contemplation with the earth cube.

10. Hold the cube in both hands and then shape the energy into another shape: a pyramid. Such as with the cube, use your imagination and hands to shape the energy.

11. Use one hand to hold the pyramid while using the other to touch the individual exposed sides, while holding it with the other.

12. Imagine that the cube transforms to red and is made of fire. Think about all the attributes of fire energy in terms of movement, heat, and the power to change.

13. Take a few moments of contemplation with the fire pyramid.

14. When you are done, absorb the energy.

15. Ground and center.

This exercise can take a lot of concentration and energy to start. If you are having problems, please stop at part 9 of the exercise and get used to shaping the energy into that of the earth. When you are ready, you can begin again to turn the earth energy into fire. If you are having problems memorizing the shapes and attributes, try doing the exercise by just changing the elemental energy, – for example, regular energy (spirit) to fire to earth but keeping it in ball form. If you are having issues with using the shapes in general, you can try using gaming dice (like those used for Dungeons and Dragons) to get a grasp of the shape structure.

Experimentation – Try going from the energy ball to the pyramid (fire) to the octahedron (air). Try going from any shape to another. Experiment with changing the elements from air to fire, to water, to earth – just using the energy in a ball (sphere).

If you have a partner, try making shapes together and concentrating on the specific energy types – learning to move the energy together in sync.

Energy does not need to be put into any sort of standard shape. The shape and quality of the energy is based upon what you are trying to accomplish and the need in the situation. I might shape the energy into a big stack of money if I wanted to do prosperity work, or I might shape it into a heart for self-love magick (how to use energy in actual spellwork will be covered later in the chapter). Next, let's try something other than geometric shapes.

Exercise #17: Energy Sculpting-Tools

1. The purpose of this exercise is to strengthen your energy manipulation skills.
2. Make an energy ball.
3. Stretch the ball out until you make the handle of a sword (feel free to look at pictures of swords beforehand).
4. With one hand, pinch the edge of the hilt and pull – lengthening the energy into the blade of the sword.
5. See and feel the weight of the sword.
6. Slowly swing it through the air – either one or two-handed.
7. Give the sword more weight, making it denser.
8. Hold the sword in one hand and feel the other end of the sword (the tip) with the other.
9. Sculpt the sword with your mind and hands. Be as detailed as possible.
10. To experiment with it, hold the sword with one hand and pass it through your other hand to "cut" it.
11. Absorb the sword when done by holding it end to end and sinking it into your personal energy, breathing it in, or any other method.

Experimentation – Try other shapes using the same template. You can make any object you can hold, or you can even create larger constructs. Play with different shapes and sizes and see what you are capable of.

Sculpting energy is once again effective, as "form follows function". The shape and quality of the energy we manipulate should be in line with the goals we are trying to accomplish. I wrote the exercise with a sword, since making tools out of energy is extremely useful, and it is a skill to master as we move forward. While physical tools are fun and capture the imagination (thus making magick easier), it is not always convenient to have a tool. Tools can be lost, damaged, or stolen – your ability to work with energy cannot.

Sending and Receiving Energy

Sending and receiving energy are probably the most natural of skills of the sorcerer. We often send energy when wishing someone "happy birthday" or if someone is asking for thoughts and prayers during a difficult time. Receiving energy is as simple as accepting a compliment or other kind word. These examples may not seem like much, but they are simple acts that can do volumes. If we think about all the energy in the Universe as like an ocean, then our magickal acts are just one drop, but every ripple in the currents of the energy of the World can create big waves if applied properly.

Energy can be sent to any person, place, or thing. It is not limited by distance or physical barriers. This is due to a few things we can learn from occult philosophy, experimentation, and theories:

Energy connects everything. Energy is a fundamental building block in all things. Just as there is a fourfold body

(See Energetic Bodies, Chapter 2) to us, there is a four-part body to every living and non-living thing. When we send energy, we are tapping into our energetic body to interact with other energetic bodies. The changes in one body affect all others.

Energy travels instantaneously. Energy travels at the speed of our thoughts and intentions. This is due partially since everything is connected, but also that energy transcends time and any limitation that it may impose normally.

Energy transcends space and matter. The realm and power of energy can be thought to be superimposed over the physical realm in a way. Modern physics tells us that most matter is made of space. How do we know that much of that space is not taken up by energy – energy that we know can be felt and changed, but that modern science just has not found a good way to measure yet?

In some ways, we are not really "sending" energy. If everything is connected, then all energy is connected. If that is true, then we are sending intentions with energy as the medium. It is still important to use energy as the medium for those intentions since we are using our minds in conjunction with the energy and the direct shaping of energy captures and utilizes the mind through the power of imagination. Without the use of our imagination, we could not send energy or do magick. Magickal techniques must engage the imagination to work effectively.

Energy is sent in two major ways. Continuous or intermittent. Energy follows many metaphors and cannot be pinned down by just one. Earlier, I compared energy to water. Now I want to use the metaphors of light. Light is usually seen as a particle or wave. As such, we can use that to categorize the two ways energy is sent: particle or continuous wave:

Particle – Think of the energy ball as a large particle of energy. Energy particles can be sent quickly for abrupt changes. The magickal dart, the energy pall, and other shaped energy that is "thrown" can be seen as particles. These are useful for the need for instant magick, quick workings, or drastic changes.

Continuous Wave – This is used for lasting changes, or things that may be done over time. As an example, your aura is a continuous wave of energy. You can do spellwork by manipulating your aura, or you may send energy in a continuous wave in a meditation. The longer the working, the more the energy will lend itself to something resembling this. For example, if a practitioner uses a doll (for love or curse work), the doll is sending out continuous waves of magickal energy.

Now let us put the theories to use.

Exercise #18: Sending Energy – Particle

1. Choose a target. This should be a three-dimensional space as far away from you as possible that you can walk to later – at least 3-10 feet (1 to 3 meters) away from you. The target itself should be a space and not a specific object. The height of the object does not matter.
2. Visualize the target area clearly.
3. Send energy to the target in a particle beam manner. This could be anything from a "magick bullet", to an energy ball, to something else. See and feel the energy before you "shoot it", then release.

4. Go to the target and feel the energy around the area. See if you can feel the shape of the target. If not, feel for the energy the same way that you would feel an aura until you get to the target area.
5. Repeat until you can go over to the energy and feel it directly. Rest and cycle your energy as needed.

Exercise #19: Sending Energy – Wave

1. Choose a target that is an object. Feel the energy of the object until you get an understanding of what it is like in its neutral state.
2. Focus on the target clearly.
3. Decide on a type of energy to send. If you do not have one, just send the energy that comes from cycling between Heaven and Earth. Send energy to the target in a wave or ray of energy.
4. Go to the target and feel the energy of the object. See if you can feel any changes.
5. Repeat until you observe a noticeable change in the energy.
6. Rest and cycle your energy as needed.

Experimentation – Try sending continuous energy from a different part of the body or a chakra (for example, Third Eye).

Energy can be sent any to non-living object and charging them is a useful skill if you want to charge water, a crystal, or really any object with energy. Sending energy to a non-living source will typically enhance the magickal properties of the object.

Exercise #20: Energy Ball Catch Game

1. This exercise needs a partner. It can be as silly or serious as you want.
2. Have each person position themselves on opposite sides of a room or outdoor area.

3. Person 1 should make an energy ball and throw it to Person 2.
4. Person 2 catches the ball, holds it, adds energy, and changes it in some manner (for example, color, texture, temperature). Person 2 throws the ball.
5. Person 1 catches the ball and repeats the process.
6. Both people catch, add, and alter the energy, and throw it back as many times as you wish.
7. Ground and center when done.

The above exercise is a great way to train. It uses our ability to manipulate energy, send, and receive it. The next exercise is to focus on receiving energy. Energy is everywhere and constantly moving. We have done some receiving of energy when we re-absorb energy balls and other energy constructs, and when we cycle energy between Earth and Heaven.

Purification

We have talked a lot about how energy can be changed – now let's talk more about types of changes. Energy can obviously be "flavored" by the user. What happens when you want to get the energy to a neutral, balanced state? When we want to do this for ourselves, we ground and center, or cycle our energy with the Earth and Heavens. We can do this also to an object or space. This is the essence of purification.

Sometimes we need an added boost to our energy work, and we call upon different sources to help us. The energy we channel for purification must suit the purpose. Typically, water energy is seen as cleansing, but often the sorcerer will cleanse with the "white light" of the Heavens.

Exercise #21: Purification of Self

1. This exercise is using "white" light to purify the self.

2. Imagine a waterfall of white light above your head. See and feel this energy as much as you can.
3. As you breathe in and out, feel the waterfall of light descending onto and through your head and neck.
4. Be aware of your breath, and let the waterfall keep going at your own pace – down and through your shoulders, arms, chest, torso, waist, legs, and feet.
5. Imagine the white light descending to the Earth – removing all stress, negativity, and impurities – and draining into and through the ground.
6. Center and take a few more deliberate breaths to close.
7. We are using the current of energy from Heaven to Earth with a more direct purpose. It is not just enough to tap into this energy, but to key in what is necessary through a direct and purposeful act.

Experimentation – Do this exercise in the shower. Try doing this exercise so that the white light descends in one breath. Let's try this exercise on something other than ourselves. The sorcerer needs to have the ability to not only purify themselves with energy, but also objects and spaces.

Exercise #22: Purification of Space
1. For this exercise, we are basically using the energy of the Heavens to cleanse a room.
2. Find a quiet indoor space with four walls.
3. Cycle your energy between Earth and Heaven.
4. See and feel the energy at the top of the room.
5. Raise your arms to the sky and energetically "feel" the ceiling and top corners of the room.
6. On your next outbreath of cycling energy from the Heavens to the Earth, imagine, see, and feel that you are bringing the energy of the Heavens to the top of the room.

7. Breathe in from the Earth to the Sky, and when you breathe out from the Heavens lower your hands in sync with your breath – from the ceiling to the ground – imagining the room is filling with white light as you do so – until they are pointing towards the ground and the entire room is filled with light.

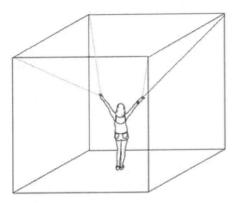

Experimentation – When you are done purifying the room, instead of just pointing your hands to the ground, try touching it. Since white light is a spectrum that contains all light – the white light of the Heavens contains all energies – try using a different color/ quality of light. An optional end to the exercise is to purify with sound as well such as a loud clap of the hands. Some magickal traditions may use an instrument such as a bell. Experimenting with different qualities of light, leads us directly to the next section on using different types of energy with our magickal interactions.

Enchantment

Enchantment is the opposite of purification in many ways. When we enchant an object or space, we are taking it from a more neutral state to the type of energy we want. There are endless techniques for this, but the following exercises will lay the groundwork for later explorations. Enchantment requires the following:

1. Something to enchant.
2. Knowledge of the type of energy you are enchanting.
3. A specific intention.

Enchantments are useful for many minor sorceries. You can enchant a coin with luck energy. A person wanting to be a better writer might enchant their pen (or keyboard). A restless person might enchant a pillow for good sleep.

Exercise #23: Enchanting an Object

1. This next exercise is going to be dependent on your specific needs and desires; as such it is more of a walkthrough of the process. Before you begin, you need an object, and a specific intention.
2. Purify the object with "white light" or any other appropriate energy, by seeing, feeling, and imagining that object filled with white light. Start at one end of the object to the other.
3. Channel the specific type of energy that goes along with your intent (this can be elemental energy such as in the chart above or a general emotion for example luck, love, etc.). Imagine it coursing through the object.
4. Think of your intent. Imagine your intent is being imprinted on the object and the energy you just channeled through the object (channeling the energy and thinking of your intent can happen at the same time).
5. Use your object appropriately with your intention.

Experimentation – Hold the object in your hand(s). See and feel any energy radiating through it. Feel the aura of the object. Hold the object and "charge" it for different lengths of time. What happens?

When most people work with charging an object, most practitioners are working with the intent or the energies they channel. It is important to do both. Sometimes we use objects that have metaphysical correspondences in alignment with our goals. This is us working with the inherent nature of the object. If you don't know the type of energy you want to use, feel free to use the "generic" energy of white light.

Energetic Alchemy – Four Step Process

The goal of the sorcerer is to make changes in the world based on the manipulation of energy. One branch of occult study that is all about making changes is alchemy. As such energy work and alchemy go hand in hand.

Alchemy is simply the occult science of transformation. This science has been used for centuries throughout the entire world and its history. A larger work on Alchemy would do it justice, but for now it is important to understand it the study of universal changes and how it is broken down into several processes. These alchemical steps can vary in number, but a general rule is that the longer the process is, the more lasting the change is. I like the 4 and 7 step process of alchemy the most, and the next section pertains to the 4-step process and how we can put any energy through an alchemical process.

The four-step process of alchemy corresponds to many "fours" in magick, such as the four energetic bodies, the 4 elements, and many more. The four-step process is as follows:

Nigredo – The Black Stage: This is the first step in the alchemical process and relates to destruction. It is said that every act of creation is an act of destruction, and that is true here. This stage corresponds to fire. It is the process of breaking down energy by destroying any previous intentions and information attached to it and reduces it to its barest essentials.

Albedo – The White Stage: This is the step of purification. This stage corresponds to water. It is said that water is the universal solvent and can absorb and wash away any impurities. Here we use the spiritual energy of water to clean the energy we reduced by fire in the last stage.

Citrinitas – The Yellow Stage: This is probably the trickiest step and is often skipped. This is realizing the inherent divinity in the energy and making a conscious choice to having that energy be reconnected to the Divine. All energy comes from the same source: The Divine or The Universe (however you want to phrase it). Here we allow the energy that is purified to shine with its own power in order to turn it over to the Universe. This phase can correspond to Air.

Rubedo – The Red Stage: The final stage is where the energy we have taken is blessed by the Divine and takes a form that we can readily change to something else or be accepted into our being. The "red stage" is a merging of the energy with ourselves, or our goals. If this energy is being used for something other than absorption into the personal energy field, then it can be used for any purpose and further transmuted based upon the will and intent of the practitioner. This stage corresponds to the Earth.

For energetic alchemy to be effective, you need to have mastered the basic trio – grounding, centering, and cycling – and the skills of absorbing energy and putting manipulating energy into the changes you want. Feel free to review *Exercise #16: Energy Shapes* and *Exercise #20: Energy Ball Catch Game*.

Exercise #24: Energetic Alchemy

1. Sit in a calm place where you will be undisturbed (optional, but useful for the first time trying this).
2. Move your arms so that your arms are off your lap, your elbows bent, and hands open as if you are receiving an object.
3. Collect the energy of the room and shape it into a pyramid.
4. See, feel, and imagine this pyramid of energy burning and slowly turning black. Imagine the energy is burned of any intention or type.
5. When you are ready, shape the energy into that of a sphere. Imagine this sphere is filled with spiritual water that can cleanse all things. Change the energy to the color white and focus on the energy being purified.
6. Keep the energy in the sphere but imagine it turning yellow. Imagine the energy glowing yellow or golden. Think of all the ways this energy is inherently good and useful. See and feel the energy stabilize and grow warmer and heavier.
7. Feel the sphere and imagine or sculpt it into a cube. See and imagine the cube turning red.
8. Let it become as solid as you can.
9. When you are ready, absorb the energy by pushing your hands together.
10. Cycle your energy.

The energy you receive can be from anywhere or anything really. I have had people "throw" bad energy at me, and I will receive it, only to take it through an alchemical process and absorb it. This is also useful for energy for spellwork.

The next chapter goes into meditation and trance so that your magick is more effective. We will also explore the astral realm, what it is, and how it pertains to modern energy magick.

Chapter 4

Meditation and Trance States

Summary: Active and Passive Meditation, Breath Work, Energy Breathing, Mantras and Words of Power, Mudras, Guided Meditations, Trance States

Getting into a deeper, and regular meditation practice, allows the practitioner to ground more into their physical body, cultivate the energy of their astral body, enjoy the expansive freedom of the mental body, and liberate them to the essential nature of the soul.

Meditation is one of the most common spiritual skills across almost every spiritual tradition. Whether as means to itself for relaxation and stress relief, or as a precursor to magickal work, the need for meditation cannot be underscored.

Active and Passive Meditation

Meditation can be broken down into two very specific categories: active and passive. Active meditation is where you are meditating specifically with intent and typically with visualizations of some sort. Passive meditations are ones where you are an observer to the processes of your body, mind, or spirit.

There is one exception to this categorization, and that is moving meditation. Moving meditation is where you are doing an activity where your body moves, but your mind is in meditation. Examples of this would be repetitive motions such as running, and walking, or even yoga. What makes it meditation is your ability to move into another mental space while doing it and the activity is the way you do it.

Since thought shapes how energy moves and is shaped, meditation is a useful tool in helping us guide energy. We have already been doing a lot of active meditation in terms of using our mind to shape energy using our sense of inner sight and imagination. Active meditation is the means in which we visualize and direct energy as we concentrate and can be used to focus the mind with a laser like quality on the task at hand.

If energy work is a sword, passive meditation is the way in which it is sharpened. Passive meditation can be used to practice clearing the mind for purposes such as stress relief and psychic maintenance, or as a way to focus away from outside influences on a specific task at hand.

Breath Work

Breath work is at the core of effective passive meditation whether you are working from schools as diverse as that of Zen Buddhism to Ceremonial Magick. Another word for magickal energy is the Sanskrit word prana, which means "breath". The connection between breath and energy is that energy, like air, is always around us and we take it in with each breath. This means that we are constantly cycling energy passively no matter what we do. CAUTION: With all breath work, try to breathe using your diaphragm, so that it is extended as you breathe in and relaxes as you breathe out. This allows more grounded breath work and helps prevent excessive lightheadedness and helps ground your breathing processes more to your body. The next exercise is to clear the mind by paying attention to this basic energy exchange in breathing.

Exercise #25: Watching the Breath
1. Set aside 5 minutes of time.
2. Sit or lie down comfortably in an undisturbed place, with your eyes open or closed.
3. Once you are comfortable, take long breaths in and out.

4. Pay attention to the way you breathe and start to breathe into a count of 5. Exhale to a count of 5 as well. Once you get into a rhythm, stop counting.

5. Let any thoughts pass by without giving them attention – put as much attention into how you breathe.

6. While this seems like a simple exercise, the challenge is to be a passive observer in your energetic processes. Energy follows attention, and by "letting go" you can take stock of your feelings and thoughts in an honest inventory. You can just be for the sake of being without worry or expectation.

Energy Breathing

As we have seen with cycling and grounding and centering, using the breath as an excuse to pay attention to our energy is very useful. You can use that same breathing to move energy in some of the following ways:

1. Literally using breath to move energy (for example, blowing an energy ball into creation instead of using your hands). This allows the practitioner to literally breathe energetic constructs into breathing or move energy so that you have your hands free.

2. "Breathing into" an object or part of the body to move energy into it. This would involve imagining that you can inhale into that object or body part to send or manipulate the energy into it.

3. Use the process of breathing to empower parts of your energetic body (for example, aura, chakras, etc.).

Tools are most effective when combined. For example, to make use of tools and subjects from earlier, you could make an energetic shield in the shape of an octahedron to add the element of air to your shield to clear out any energy coming your way from miscommunication or gossip.

The following exercise comes in part from kundalini yoga, but there is a noticeably Pagan spin on it by working with visualization and shaping the energy directly. This is a good exercise to empower yourself before any magickal working or to charge yourself up when you need a boost of energy. CAUTION: If you feel lightheaded or if you are going to pass out, please stop immediately.

Exercise #26: Breath of Fire

1. Ground and center.
2. With your eyes open or closed – breathe in and out, taking time to take long breaths and let your breathing
3. As you breathe, cycle your energy.
4. Surround yourself with the raw element of Fire by visualizing that the energy around you is turning red, or the colors of fire. See and feel the fiery energy around you.
5. Breathe in the fiery energy through your nose, and exhale through your mouth. As you breathe in, cycle the energy into and through you. The energy should flow in, circulate, and go out in one breath.
6. Once you can circulate the elemental energy, breathe in normally – or to a count of three – and exhale as quickly as possible.
7. Continue until you feel filled up with as much fire energy as possible.
8. Gradually return to normal breathing and absorb the energy into your center, and ground as needed.

The above exercise can be used with any specific energies (for example, lunar and solar) that you wish to charge yourself with. You can use really any type of archetypal energy – anything from astrological and planetary energies to runes or even the forces of the tarot. The next exercise uses breath work to charge your energetic centers as they relate to the four bodies. If you remember the four main parts of the body are the physical, astral, mental, and soul. Looking at the chart below, we can add some other correspondences:

Body	Celestial Energy or Realm	Corresponding Physical Location
Physical	Earth or Terrestrial	Feet
Astral	Moon or Astral	Belly or Center
Mental	Sun or Solar	Heart
Soul	Stars or Stellar	Head

These correspondences are meant to be guides. For example, if you want to connect more to your dreams and emotions, which correspond to the astral, you could focus more on that energy center or on meditation/breath work with lunar energies. This set of correspondences will come back into play in Chapter 10 when we talk about spiritual journeying.

Exercise #27: Energizing the Self

1. If possible, please stand for this exercise (if not, sitting would be more appropriate than lying down).
2. Breathe in and out in a relaxed manner.
3. Imagine, see, and feel the energy of the Earth below you.
4. Breathe in through the Earth and breathe out through your feet. As you breathe in and out cycle your energy in a constant current between the two. Do this for as many breaths as you need.
5. Breathe in and out of your feet to energize and charge them.
6. On your next inhale, breathe from the Earth, through your feet, and to your belly or center.
7. Exhale from your center, through your feet, and to the Earth. Cycle your energy back and forth between the Earth, through your feet and center, and back again.

8. Breathe in and out of your center to energize and charge them.
9. Repeat this process for your heart and head.
10. When you have breathed in and out of your head, cycle your energy from the Earth to the Heavens – making sure you are concentrating on the various energy centers.
11. Center to complete the exercise. Ground if needed.

Experimentation – Try doing this exercise from the top down, starting in the Heavens/crown chakra, and descending to the Earth/foot chakras.

Mantras and Words of Power

Mantras have been used in meditation for thousands of years. It is typically a word containing spiritual significance or power. In meditation, mantras have a dual purpose. The primary purpose is a focus point of attention. They give the mind something to direct its attention on and help focus an intent (for example, a healing mantra might be repeated in order to facilitate recovery from an illness). Since energy is directed by attention, using a mantra is a simple yet effective tool to help focus that attention and direct the intention of your energy.

The secondary purpose of a mantra is to help go into different states of consciousness. The more someone can chant a mantra, the more it is possible to go into a deeper state of relaxation and deep trance. The deeper the meditation and trance, the more effective magick can be.

Mantras can also be words of power. When we use a word, it can be seen as a container for meaning. For example, the word "cat" will conjure images of all sorts of cats from your life experience and knowledge base. In a similar manner, words of power are containers for magickal and spiritual energies. Since words of power that have been used for long periods of time seem to retain some energy from those that have used them, and they are in and of themselves energetic magickal creations, they have a sort of vitality on their own. This should not discourage the practitioner from creating their own words of power (which will be covered in the next chapter on sigils). *Magick Words: A Dictionary*, by Craig Conley, is a great resource for this.

To make words of power even more effective, I like to charge up my throat chakra by cycling energy to it breathing in and out of it. This is like a standard opening of the chakra, except that I am actively pushing more energy into that chakra, and very much like opening the hand chakras from earlier. It is also possible to alternate between cycling energy between the throat chakra and the mouth directly to open and charge the channel between the two.

Any word or string of words can be used for magickal works. What really makes it magickal, is your ability to go to a special state of consciousness that is not of the ordinary world and stirs the emotions, imagination, and will.

Mantras and words of power are ways to move and shape energy. In Exercise #11, when we talked about the personal shield, you were asked to use a word of power to help shape and direct the energy of your personal shield. I advise creating your own dictionary of words of power to aid your regular practice and help direct energy for any purpose. The more of your senses you engage in magickal work, the more effective it is.

Exercise #28: Abracadabra

Abracadabra is an old word of power. It is from the Aramaic phrase "avra kehdabra" that means, "I will create as I speak". This is a great general-purpose word of power since it allows you to focus your attention and make the intentions manifest into reality. For this exercise, think of a specific energy or intention that you want to manifest.

1. Ground and center.
2. Get into a relaxed pose, sitting or lying down. Take slow deep breaths, and on the exhale begin to recite Abracadabra.
3. Start saying the word faster and faster. Imagine that your energy is building with each time you say the word. If you are visualizing something to go with your magickal intent, see that image become clearer and clearer.
4. When you have chanted as fast as you can, with as much energy and intent as possible, release it. If you need a "target" for your energy, either use the Heavens or the Earth.
5. To bring your energy back to normal, start chanting slower and slower until you get to a regular breathing pattern.
6. Ground and center.

In this exercise, the building of energy to reach a climax and release is called a "cone of power" by some practitioners. In the cone they may visualize the energy spiraling upwards to point to be released. There are three main philosophies on where you should release the energy:

To the Heavens/The Universe – The idea is that you are sending the energetic intent to the Universe, or even the gods, to become manifest.

To the Earth – The main point would be to send the energy to the Earth to manifest, in the similar manner of putting a seed in the ground.

Internal/External – The energy can be taken internally to empower or to extend outwards. If the energy goes outward this is to the effect that everything is connected, and you are making an energetic "ripple" to affect change in the world you are connected to.

Words of power can be used in singular workings, or repeated everyday as part of a daily meditation practice. Using them energetically is magickal working by themselves. The magickal words can also be combined to make a "magickal sentence". For example, in the invocation to the deity Pan, "Io Pan", is the combination of two words "io" and "Pan". Io, a Greek word used in magick for the purpose of invocation (drawing an energy into yourself), is the verb and Pan (the deity of wild nature) is the noun. Combined, they shape and manifest the intent of drawing the deity down.

One of the most popular words of power is the runes of the ancient Norse. The runes were the main alphabet of the Germanic peoples, and there is much evidence that they were used for magickal purposes. Each letter of the runic alphabet has symbolism attached that can be used for magick and divination. One of the magickal purposes was what was called galdr, or a type of magickal singing of a runic incantation. While traditional galdr involves singing magickal phrases in a specific manner, we can work something similar by singing a rune to invoke its energy. This can be used as part of a ritual, a ritual by itself, or even as a preliminary act to ready oneself for magickal work.

For the next exercise you can pick a rune from a catalog of runes (I would recommend Diana L. Paxson's *Taking Up the Runes*), but for the sake of this exercise, let us use the rune Gebo. Gebo is a rune that means "gift" and looks like the letter "x". It has ties to the Norse virtue of hospitality and speaks to gratitude, and the positive aspects of giving and receiving. In magickal work, this might be used to express gratitude or thanksgiving. Working with Gebo, I feel it in my heart, and I feel gratitude for what I have received, and it helps foster the love that comes with the virtue of generosity. When singing or chanting a rune (or any word of power), we are using the breath we are expending as well as our mind's focused on that specific word to actually shape energy. In this case the energy we are shaping is that which is around us and through us. The purpose could be to empower our energies and lives with that specific runic energy, or as a way of bringing that type of energy closer to our lives for our own personal transformation.

Exercise #29: *Rune Singing (Using Gebo)*

1. Take deep breaths to get into a meditative state with your eyes opened or closed.
2. Breathe in slowly, and slowly sing out the rune Gebo (pronounced "gay-boo"). Make sure you are taking the time to draw out the syllables as long as possible. If it helps, you can make the first syllable higher than the second.
3. Sing the rune for several more times until you get into a rhythm.
4. Visualize the rune over you, if you wish.
5. Let your singing get more and more intense until it reaches its climax.
6. Ground the energy into your heart or center.

I personally like to keep words of power somewhat simple so that I can use visualization and breath work in conjunction with them. For example, if I was doing healing work directly on a person, I might chant a personal word of power while visualizing the healing recipient as healthy and the ailment fading. The more intense I chant, the more I go into trance to make more lasting effects and the more intense I let myself visualize the positive outcome. The word of power is shaping the outcome, but it is also shaping the energy of my awareness.

Mudras

We are conductors for magickal energy, and the way we shape our bodies can change how that energy is conducted. This is one of many reasons why some mystical schools place great importance on posture in meditation. We have seen that energy can be shaped by intention, thought, visualization, and breath – movement is another way to move, direct, and manipulate energy. While physical movement is a wonderful way to raise and affect energy, this next section talks about gestures the body can make while still to direct and influence the energy you use.

Mudras are basically symbolic hand gestures that can be used for meditation, magick, or communication. They originate in Indian yoga and magick but are also used in performances such as plays and dances. Mudras are ways to conduct, direct, and harness energy. Coming from the schools of Indian yoga and magick, the five elements can correspond to the five fingers on the hand. By focusing on a specific hand gesture that highlights a specific finger, we can tap into elemental energies in a more direct way. These gestures can invoke the element, and they can also transform energy that you harness. To use the mudra, use your thumb to hold down the indicated finger. For example, for the Air mudra you would use your thumb to hold down your index finger.

Air/Index finger

Fire/Thumb

Water/Little finger

Earth/Ring finger

Spirit/Middle finger

Exercise #30: Receiving Energy with Mudras (Akasha)

1. Sit and relax in a safe space where you will be undisturbed.
2. Make the "spirit" mudra with both hands.
3. Hold your hands apart so that your fingertips are pointing at a singular area.
4. Turn your hands so your palms are facing each other.
5. Breathe in and out. See and feel the energy collecting from the place you are, to the area that your fingertips are pointing.

6. Breathe in and out. See and feel that energy move from where it was collecting, to inside your hands, through your arms, and to the rest of your body.
7. Do a closed circulation of the energy.
8. Keep meditating on the energy that is flowing from the room to you, through the mudra. Do this until you can cycle your energy while also receiving energy.

I used to have problems receiving energy. I used to try to suck it into me as if I had an energetic straw. It took me a long time to realize that energy is constantly flowing in and out of us, and accepting it is fairly easy because I was working with the nature of dynamic that was already there. Circulating the energy you receive is the best thing to do, since our energetic organs get a chance to process it and make it directly accessible.

While in the last exercise you basically observed how the mudra can shape energy passively. Here are some ways to try experimenting with different effects with the mudras more actively:

Use the Air mudra in conjunction with your Third eye to clear it and create a better sense of incoming communication for divination.

1. Use the Earth mudra to help you ground.
2. Use the Earth mudra in energy healing over a healing recipient when trying to promote the physical body's natural healing mechanisms.
3. Try the Fire mudra while visualizing and charging your personal shield.
4. Use the Water mudra to enchant and charge water, with your hand above the water.

You can also come up with your own mudras by experimenting with the correspondences of the fingers and elements. For example, I have made a triangle with the thumbs and index fingers of my both hands touching. This gesture not only uses the thumb (fire), but it creates an energetic circuit. It also helps that a symbol for fire in Western magick is the upright triangle.

Guided Meditations

A guided meditation is usually an active meditation that is guided by someone else. This can be in person or recorded. Many of the exercises in this book function as a type of guided meditation where I am trying to lead you to a specific image, effect, or feeling. I often use guided meditations that help me access different realms which we will cover in "Chapter 10: Trance Journeying", but also for anything needed for my personal energy. The following meditation is intended to guide you through the transformation of the energy of the four major elements as they reside within you archetypically.

Exercise #31: Guided Meditation – Elemental Transformation

Record or have someone read the following meditation. The meditation should be read slowly, and between paragraphs allow at least a 30 second pause.

Ground and center, and let your mind relax more and more as you hear the meditation.

Meditation Text

With your eyes open or closed, let your attention come to your breathing. Breathe in and out – letting your breathing become slower and deeper. Let each breath carry you deeper into a state of relaxation, deeper into a state of meditation. Let the sound of my voice and any other sounds bring you deeper and deeper into a state of relaxation.

When you are in as deep a state of meditation as possible, imagine you are breathing in air, not just breath, but the pure energies of the Air element. See and feel the element that you are breathing in. What color is it? What does it feel like in your body as you breathe it in?

As you breathe in and out, imagine the energy becoming warmer and warmer. See, feel, and imagine the energies of Air slowly become those of Fire as you breathe in and out. Let these energies flow into you and out of you with every inhale and exhale. What color is that fiery energy? How does it make you feel? What colors do you see? As you breathe in and out, attune yourself with the energies of Fire.

As you breathe in and out, imagine the energy becoming cooler and cooler; heavier and heavier. See, feel, and imagine the energies of Fire slowly become those of Water as you breathe in and out. Let these energies flow into you and out of you with every inhale and exhale. What color is that water energy? How does it flow? How does it make you feel? What colors do you see? As you breathe in and out, attune yourself with the energies of Water.

Breathing in and out, imagine the energy becoming drier and drier, heavier and heavier. See, feel, and imagine the energies of Water slowly become those of Earth as you breathe in and out. Let these energies sink into you and ground you with every inhale and exhale. What color is that earth energy? How does it make you feel? What colors do you see? As you breathe in and out, attune yourself with the energies of Earth.

Breathing in and out, focus on your physical body. Notice the energy of your feet, your legs, and hips. Pay attention to the feelings in your belly, your chest, arms, and hands. Feel how solid your neck, jaw, and head are. Slowly open your eyes if they are closed – coming back to this time and place.

Trance States

What makes guided meditation so effective is your ability to go into trance. Trance is an altered state of consciousness, where there are many levels. I think of it as a spectrum between being awake and dreaming. Knowledge of the different trances is useful since the deeper the state of trance that one can get into while doing magickal work, the deeper the effects. The different brainwave states are:

Gamma – Concentration, the state of being where the mind is learning and problem solving.

Beta – Wakeful State, this is "normal" alert consciousness where the mind is active.

Alpha – Meditation, the state of consciousness where the mind is relaxed.

Theta – Deep Trance, the in-between state where the mind is both awake and is in deepest meditation.

Delta – Dreaming, the deepest state of consciousness where the outside senses nearly shut down.

Throughout the course of this work, we have dealt mainly with the alpha state of consciousness. If we can move energy past alpha to theta while we visualize, move, and shape energy it will be more effective. This does not mean that you should only work with energy in theta, but to emphasize the extra power you can lend to your magick. The next exercise is a means to bridge the gap between alpha and theta by riding one state of consciousness to get to another. It can be done with or without music.

Exercise #32: Trance Dance
1. Stand comfortably with some space between your feet.
2. Pay attention to your breath as you breathe in and out.
3. Start to sway back and forth. As you breathe in and out, and the more you relax and get deeper into trance, let

your movements become rhythmic. You can start with the extremities such as the hands, arms, feet, shoulders, and head.

4. As you breathe in and out and your movements become more and more rhythmic, let your thoughts flow in and out of your mind – focusing more on your movements and breathing.

5. Stop thinking about your breathing and focus on your movements – letting them get more and more rhythmic and intense.

6. Let your thoughts and movements flow spontaneously until they reach a climax.

7. Let your movements and breathing relax and get slower and slower.

8. Ground and center

In the above exercise you may have noticed that you're breathing and movements almost took on a life of their own. You're breathing and movements became a way for your conscious mind to let go. It is in letting go that deeper magick can occur. If I was using trance dance to move energy, I would have an intention that I would want to manifest, use my breathing and movement to raise energy, and let that energy go to complete the working. Once you get used to different trance states, especially alpha and theta, you can attempt to consciously move energy and attention to an unconscious place. Delta consciousness would be the realm of Dream work and lucid dreaming which would entail a completely different work to cover.

If we look at our correspondences between the different energetic bodies, we could almost map how they would associate with different states of consciousness. The beta, or wakeful state would, correspond to the physical body with its focus on the material world. Alpha consciousness would correspond with the astral realm, especially since it is in this state of weekend meditation; we typically move energy the most. The theta state would be the best State of Consciousness to access the deepest aspects of the mental self. Finally, the delta state would be the access point of which we could enter purely spiritual consciousness.

Whether you are sitting, standing, or moving you can get into a state of meditation. It is in this place of letting go – these in between or liminal – that working with energy is the most effective and magickal.

Chapter 5

Sigils

Summary: What is a Sigil? Sacred Geometry and Numerology, Popular Sigils in Magick, Sigils in Nature, Creating Personal Sigils, Hyper Sigils

What Is a Sigil?

Sigils, like words of power, are receptacles for magickal energy and intention but they are visual instead of auditory. This includes everything from the standard pentacle to astrological signs and runes. Sigils are particularly effective since they act on most aspects of consciousness at once. Sigils, like mudras, give us new ways to shape energy through how it is conducted, while the sigils themselves can be used to manipulate energy by virtue of their meaning. Thought shapes energy, and since sigils can be containers of psychic energy, the mental energy inherent in a sigil can help us manipulate what we wish. There is a two-way relationship happening here: the sigils are given meaning by our experience, and our consciousness is shaped by the sigils.

Sigils do not have to be from a traditional or historical magickal alphabet. The most common sigils are born out of a way to describe a psychic or mystic force. In this fashion they function as an expression of where personal consciousness meets pure Spirit and become a sort of mystical art form. The occultist, Austin Osman Spare, spoke to this when he said, "Art is the instinctive application of the knowledge latent in the subconscious". What he meant is that art helps reveal the hidden, the "occult". Sometimes the place it is revealed from is the deepest aspects of our mind, but sometimes it draws upon the subtle world that only mystics dare to tread.

Although most sigils are two-dimensional, energy can be felt in at least three dimensions. Energetic sigils can be inscribed onto or within, someone or something, as well as sent out to the place of your choosing. Imagine banishing someone with a sigil to ward them off or marking a place to stop someone from being there. I had a teacher that would send protective energy to her door, and people would literally almost bounce off it. This is due to the amount of energy, how it is shaped, will power, and imagination.

Exercise #33: Feeling the Pentacle

1. Prepare yourself to manipulate energy. Opening the hand chakras would be a good exercise for this.
2. Cycle your energy (so you are not taxing your own personal energy too much).
3. With one hand, a finger, or a mudra, trace a five-pointed star in the air (pictured).
4. With the other hand, feel the surface of the pentacle.
5. See and feel the pentacle have different colors (for example, elemental colors, black, or white) and see what changes occur.
6. Absorb the energy of the pentacle when complete, and ground.

Experiment: Hold the pentacle and manipulate it as you would move an energy ball back and forth from place to place.

In some schools of ceremonial magick, instead of calling the quarters like in a Wiccan circle, pentacles of each element are used to consecrate the space (for example, pentacle of air, pentacle of fire, etc.). By tapping into the egregore (collective psychic energy) of this, you can use the pentacle to banish or invoke elemental and other energies. You can get creative such as using an energetic black pentacle on a toxic neighbor's door to cause them to move away while visualizing them leaving your neighborhood (with the intention they are moving for a "good" reason).

Sigils can be used within the energetic body also. Imagine inscribing a green, Earth pentacle inside someone and doing healing energy work on them. My favorite use of sigils and energetic body is to implant them in the aura directly for purposes such as protection.

Exercise #34: *Implanting Runes in the Aura (Algiz)*
Runes can be thought of to be sigils from the Norse tradition. They were used as an alphabet, and for magickal uses. The Norse rune Algiz (pronounced "al-jiz") has the lore of being extremely protective. Before getting started, practice tracing the Algiz rune (pictured) in the air. Also practice making the sound of the rune by singing it, toning it out, or speaking it in a rhythmic manner.

1. Ground, center, and clear your aura with energy.
2. Feel around in your aura for a good place to put the rune in your energetic field.
3. Inscribe the rune in your aura while speaking it aloud.
4. Feel for the changes in your aura. What changes? How does this make you feel?

This technique can be used multiple times in your aura. I would advise on using runes, or other sigils, that you find as positive, supportive, protective, or healing as much as possible. On a side note, the Norse runes can be associated with different deities, so take care in choosing runes that are either not associated with a deity, or with ones you want to align with.

Sigils and symbols in general, can be used with a focus as a mnemonic device. Mnemonic devices serve as ways to remember the things you associate with them. In the Western Kabalistic tradition (ceremonial magick combined with Jewish mysticism), each letter of the Hebrew alphabet corresponds with a card of the major arcana of Tarot. The High Priestess card symbolizes secrets, mystery, and intuition. Let us say we want to easily access the power of the tarot to manipulate energy, we could tap into the Hebrew letter as a sigil representing the High Priestess.

Exercise #35: Visualizing and Cycling Sigil Energy (Gimel)

1. Center to be aware of your personal energy.
2. In the middle of the room you are in, draw Gimel (pictured).
3. Step away from the sigil and either sit or stand some distance from the sigil.
4. Imagine the sigil radiating the energy of the High Priestess, or if you are unfamiliar with tarot, the energy of mysteries, secrets, and initiation.
5. As you watch your breath, imagine, and feel you are taking in that energy.
6. Cycle the energy between you and the sigil.
7. Let the energy course through and within you for a few minutes.

8. When you are done, center, absorb the energy of the sigil and ground.

When we use a Sigil with energy behind it, we are activating its potential. In the above exercise, you could have said the Hebrew letter aloud as you made it in the air, but that is not completely necessary, but it will add extra power to your work as you are using more of your senses to channel your will and magickal imagination. Research different Hebrew letters and their correspondence to the Tarot. Experiment with getting to know the Tarot in this manner and see how it makes you feel.

Sacred Geometry and Numerology

Some sigils fall into, and are created by, more structured models. Shapes are everywhere and the mathematical study of shapes is geometry. We can expand our study of shapes into the sacred and talk about sacred geometry where pattern meets spiritual meaning. Some geometrical shapes have both an inscribed and assigned meaning. There is an idea in occult teachings that some things have an inherent property, and here we will talk about those inherent qualities of shapes and numbers. Shapes and numbers can also be combined into codified structures that we call magick squares.

Many sigils can be broken down into simpler shapes, but those simpler shapes form a bit of a visual alphabet that we can draw upon. Below are some shapes that form the basis of many sigils.

Horizontal Line: Earth, or the terrestrial plane

Vertical Line: Heaven, the spiritual plane,
or the path between Spirit and Earth

Cross: Earth, matter, manifestation

Circle: Pure Spirit, or the Soul

Semi-Circle/Crescent: Spiritual Energy, Collecting

Arrow: Movement

Upward Triangle: Liberation of Energy
(Earth traveling to Spirit)

Downward Triangle: Manifestation of energy
(Spirit traveling to Earth)

Square: Solidification of energy into form

Using the above shapes, I could make a sigil that would be like the one pictured. Using the key above, it looks like I made a sigil that represents the liberation of energy into the realm of pure spirit by combining the upward triangle, vertical line, and circle.

This might be a good sigil for letting things go to Spirit, or if I was trying to release unwanted energy to Spirit. Another interpretation would be that I am giving energy to Spirit or the Gods, in the sense of an offering. One could make this sign energetically over an offering or inscribe the energy directly inside of what is offered. Conversely, this symbol could be used if I wanted to have an experience in meditation where I am trying to attune more with energies of "the Above" or pure Spirit. Take some time to play with the symbols above and see what you can come up with.

Exercise #36: Experimentation

1. Take time to meditate on each of the above shapes.
2. Decide on a magickal intention or goal.

3. Use the shapes to make your own sigil based upon that intention or goal.
4. Meditate on that sigil to feel how the sigil matches the intention.

I could probably keep going on this on the above chart and expand into pentagons, hexagons, septagons, and many more. From here we can expand into how numbers are used in magick in the sacred science numerology, or the mystical symbolism of numbers. As shapes have spiritual symbolism and meaning, as do numbers. Below is a chart on some common number symbolism. Think of the below as a sample guide to numerology. If we bring number and shape together, we deepen our connection to the magickal forces we draw upon, and we can create more complex works of functional magickal art. Below is some basic numerology to add to the sigil making tools. This is just a small sample.

One – Independence, Wholeness
Two – Duality
Three – Change, the Triple Goddess, Transformation
Four – Stability, The Four Seasons, Manifestation, The four bodies / the 4 realms
Five – Motion, Five Elements, Spiritual Mysteries
Six – Harmony
Seven – Spirituality, the days of the week, seven classical planets, Seven chakras
Eight – Initiation, Abundance, the Wheel of the Year, Infinity
Nine – Completion, The nine Norse realms
Ten – Coming full cycle, The 10 sefirot on the Kabbalistic Tree of Life

Taking number and shape into account, let us say I want to create a sigil for having good luck at a job interview. I might also want to draw in forces of good luck and financial prosperity. I might make something like what is pictured. The downward triangle represents the manifestation of the magickal intent. The four-sided square represents job stability. The arrow represents quick movement.

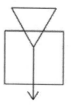

Popular Sigils in Magick

In modern magick, there are a host of popular sigils for the elements, astrology, runes, and much more. Color symbolism can be combined in any sigil. One of the most popular symbols sets is that of the four elements. A traditional way of depicting the four elements is through the symbol set below. As you can see, I subtly added the sigil for Earth (corresponding to the physical realm, finances, fertility, etc.) to my last example.

Air

Fire

Water

Earth

These symbols have been used for thousands of years since the time of the ancient Greeks and through the ages. For the next exercise, we are going to use sigils in the practical magickal purpose of calling the four elements for magickal work. While we will go over creating sacred/ceremonial space in the next chapter, I wanted to talk about how we can use sigil sets in a common magickal practice.

Exercise #37: Calling the Four Quarters with Sigils

1. Ground and center. Purify the room with energy.
2. Meditate on the element of Air and how and where it exists within you and outside of you.
3. Start in the east and draw the Air sigil in that direction at the edge of your space. Visualize and feel the sigil being made of Air energy as you trace the symbol in the air.
4. Go to the south, meditate on the Fire elemental energy within and outside of you, and then draw the sigil in Fire the air.
5. Repeat with Water in the west and Earth in the north.
6. Go back to the east, feel the energy of the sigils upon you and radiating outwards. Meditate upon this feeling.
7. When finished, absorb the energy of the elements by feeling for the sigil's energy in the air and take it within yourself. Start in any order that feels right energetically/intuitively.
8. Center and ground.

The preceding exercise can be done with or without words. If you are working with a group, experiment on how it feels when different people summon various elements.

Another popular symbol set using basic shapes above is the symbols that correspond to the planets. For the sake of keeping things concise, I want to focus on the seven classical planets of the ancients – the stellar bodies that were visible of ancient mystics and occultists.

☉

The Sun: Harmony, Balance, Life Giving Energy,
Illumination, Truth, Celebration

☾

The Moon: Emotions, the Astral, Mystery,
the Hidden, Intuition

♀

Venus: Love, Sex, Romance, Attraction, Beauty

♂

Mars: Warrior Energy, Violence, Aggression,
Force, Determination, Vigilance

☿

Mercury: Communication, Eloquence, Travel,
Business, Crossing Boundaries

♃

Jupiter: Expansion, Generosity, Luck,
Leadership, Charisma

♄

Saturn: Boundaries, Death, Time, Endings, Change

By meditation on the component shape meanings and the symbol, we can find greater mysteries. For example, in the symbol for Mars we can see the circle (spiritual energy) and the arrow (movement) combine to speak to a sort of understanding that pure force comes from a movement of spiritual energy. I will leave you to formulate your own truths, but I want to drive home the point on how symbols combine with others in greater complexity. It is in this complexity that we can create magick that is greater and more effective than the sum of its parts.

In magick, sometimes great energy is created in the union of opposites much in the way that electricity is created with the interaction of positive and negative forces. The energy of the planets above can be seen in three opposing pairs (Sun and Moon, Venus and Mars, Jupiter, and Saturn), with Mercury being complete unto itself. The illuminating power of the Sun comes into contrast with the hidden powers of the Moon; the love and beauty of Venus can be seen as a polar opposite of the violent Energies of Mars, while the expansion of Jupiter comes square against the boundaries of Saturn. The planetary powers of Mercury can cross the boundary by their very nature. The next exercise calls us to hold polar opposite energies in contrast to each other to generate magickal force.

Exercise #38: Holding Paradox (Mars and Venus)

1. Center.
2. Memorize the correspondences of the planetary forces above and choose a pair to work with.
3. Meditate upon the planetary energy of Venus. Draw it sigil in front of you. Meditate upon it and draw its energies into you – seeing and feeling it as much as possible. When you are filled with the energy of Venus as much as possible, absorb the sigil into yourself, and center.
4. Repeat the process with the energy of Mars.

5. Hold out your hands with your palms up, and visualize the sigil of Venus in one hand and Mars in the other. Alternatively, you can draw each sigil in the air with your finger and place your hand at the bottom of each sigil as if you were holding them up.

6. Change the position of how you energetically hold the sigils, so your hands move from the bottom of the sigils to the sides.

7. Bring your hands closer together to combine the sigils energetically.

8. Feel the energies combine into a ball, let the visualization of the energies relax, and allow the energies to grow stronger and more vibrant.

9. Hold on to this energy ball for as long as possible. When ready, release it to the Heavens.

10. Ground and center.

I like to use this exercise when I need more magick that is more intense or to power things such as energetic constructs and artificial spirits – semi-independent machines made of energy that accomplish specific goals. Just as electricity is generated by the interaction of two polar opposite forces, we can use polarity in magick in a similar fashion.

Sigils in Nature

For those that are willing, sigils can appear anywhere. The last sets of sigils come from schools of mysticism or spiritual experience. When a spiritual practitioner has a deep experience, and makes art, that art is imbued with the energy of that experience. A certain kind of magick occurs when we observe something with spiritual power, and for those that follow an Earth based religion, the most powerful thing that can exist for some is the Earth.

Sigils are abundant in Nature. A flower created by the magick of photosynthesis is a natural sigil for the Sun. There are patterns and shapes in the growth of trees (see the pentacle drawn over the maple leaf pictured), and the gnarled geometry branches. In a seashell is the "golden ratio" of infinity, while we see the pentacle in the starfish. Sigils from Nature can bring the natural world to us in magick so that we can draw upon it, and it opens us up to the rich experience that happens when our soul meets the manifested world in its raw form. This next exercise does require something to write on and something to write with.

Exercise #39: Sigils in Nature

1. Go outside and journey until you find something in Nature that has a pattern or shape. 2. Conversely, you can find a natural object or a picture of one.
2. Meditate on that shape. After you have taken a few minutes, write down any thoughts, feelings, or impressions.
3. Draw a sigil based on the chosen shape.

You can repeat this exercise to make an entire "magickal alphabet", personal divination set, or just a library of natural energies to be used for later use. This technique can be used from any natural source for any magickal purpose. For example, one could take the shape of leaves from magickal herbs to create a sigil or use the protective properties of a seashell.

Creating Personal Sigils

Sigils can be as personal and specific as you need. Sometimes you want to use something that is more targeted, personal, or customized to the situation. Peter J. Carroll in his work *Liber Null and Psychonaut* outlines a technique of magickal reduction that is effective in creating both a personalized sigil and a word of power. The first requirement is to have a magickal intent that is specific. For example, "I want to have more joy in my life." The reduction technique would take that phrase and delete any repeating letters, and you would get something like the below.

I WANT TO HAVE MORE JOY IN MY LIFE.
I WANT O H VE M R J Y I L F

From there, you have the letters I, W, A, N, T, O, H, V, E, M, R, J, Y, I, L, AND F. To make a word of power use your intuition and personal preferences and inclinations rearrange the letters into something somewhat nonsensical and somewhat magickal. For my example, I came up with the below.

I W A N T O H V E M R J Y I L F
TANWI OHVEM FILJYR

For the sigil aspect, you want to take the letters and use them to make a sigil. This may take several phases. The first phase is to just get the letters down, the second phase is to smooth the sigil out and make it less clunky, and the third stage is to refine it for use. Using the unique letters, I came up with the following.

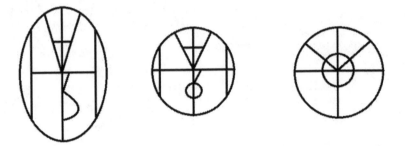

The idea is to reduce something complex to something simple and iconic that stirs the imagination and is easy enough to memorize.

Exercise #40: Using a Sigil and Word of Power

1. Make a sigil and a word of power based on the above "reduction" technique. Memorize the sigil or have it drawn on a piece of paper and put it within your view so that you can reference the drawing.
2. Ground, center, and purify the space.
3. Gather energy by cycling. Alternatively, you can open your hand chakras.
4. Draw the sigil in the air. At the same time speak your word of power so that you are exhaling energy into the sigil. Draw out the syllables of your word of power as you speak it.

Option #1: If it is directed at a person, hold the sigil by connecting to the energy of the sigil with an open hand, pause to reflect, and then when you exhale – throw the energy towards your target while imagining the sigil and its energy are being sent to that person.

Option #2: Hold the sigil with both hands and breathe so that you are exhaling faster than you inhale almost as if you are hyperventilating. When your breathing is as intense as possible and you have raised enough energy through this process, send the sigil to the Universe/God(s)/Spirit, to the Earth, or outwards from you as you see fit.

There is much debate in magickal circles about whether energy raised in magick should be directed towards the Heavens, the Earth, or outwards to manifest your goal. I have found better luck with sending the energy to the Heavens so that my higher powers – whether it is the ancestors, the gods, or the Universe – know my intent and can direct that energy to where it needs to go. Since everything is connected energetically, sending the magickal energy we raise makes an energetic ripple in the collective pond of the energy we are all a part of. Another school of thought is that the energy we send to the Earth acts like a seed to grow our desires into results we can harvest. I will leave it to you to figure out what works best for you, and I encourage constant practice and experimentation.

Hyper Sigils

Sigils can be combined for greater complexity. Complex and multilayered sigils that combine several symbols into one are called hyper sigils. Using the examples from above, I can focus my magickal intent more precisely. Let us say that I want a sigil to incorporate something positive like mental health and self-love into my life. I might make a beginning sigil like the one pictured where Spirit is manifesting to my soul.

Already I have the sign for water incorporated. Since I specifically want to add love into my life, I can add the sign for Venus in the "Spirit" and "soul" part of my sigil to represent the outpouring of Universal love to the self.

We can also combine this with any other words, images, or symbols that would be appropriate. I would say that the rule of thumb should be sigils that you can easily commit to memory. While writing something down in magick and reciting it (in this case taking a written sigil and inscribing it) is effective, the power behind it is magnified when it is committed to memory and internalized.

Using our job interview sigil from above, we can use the money symbol to make it a hyper sigil very easily. Do not hesitate to incorporate any symbol that has meaning, energetic charge, or significance. The only warning is that if you are using sigils that are not of the "common use", just be careful where they are coming from and what they are charged with.

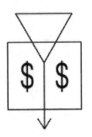

I would say that sigils can be as elaborate as you want, but part of the magick of sigils comes in their ability, as visual art, to shift our consciousness. It is very possible to over think a sigil to the point that you will not be able to fall into at least a state of relaxation that is the bare minimum to engage in magickal acts. This over thinking can work against you. To use a metaphor, if you were cooking something you do not want to undercook or overcook it – you want to get it just right.

You can use the techniques above in creating sigils for other magickal work. A sigil can be inscribed on magickal objects (such as a candle for candle magick), or even drawn on magickal objects. Typically, sigils, in non-energy work need to be charged first before use but we are making sigils with energy so that step is not necessary. For energetic magick, you can inscribe a sigil inside the aura of the object you want to enchant, or directly inside of something by visualizing the energy under the surface.

If you do want to charge a sigil for extra effect you can use a technique like the "breath of fire" – from *Exercise #26* – where you breathe out faster than you inhale, almost like you are hyperventilating – and use the energy raised to "super charge" the sigil to an even greater effect.

Chapter 6

Sacred and Ceremonial Space

Summary: Banishment, Warding, Circle Casting, Cosmology and Astrology, Blessing

Creating sacred space is something that is common in many spiritual and mystical traditions. Whether you are casting a circle and calling the elements, to something simple such as burning incense or ringing a bell, making a physical space ready for spiritual work is useful to get into the energetic and mental space of getting to work. It is about setting the stage and creating a solid energetic foundation to do your magickal work.

Banishment

Energy is everywhere. Have you ever gone into a room where someone has argued or had a bad fight? The energy of the room feels different. You can almost feel all the tension and pain that is going on. Well energetically cleansing the space as a scribe in a previous chapter is extremely useful, there are sometimes stronger energetic forces that we need to deal with. When doing magick, a physical space should be in a neutral state, and we need to be more aggressive and how we deal with it to get there. Banishment is the magickal art I'm getting rid of unwanted energies in a direct manner.

There are many ways to banish energy. You can use words of breath, words of power, sigils, or just sending your energy outside of yourself to displace unwanted energies – or in some cases spirits or other entities. The typical idea is as follows:

1. Gather energy.
2. Direct energy at the target to displace or disperse it.
3. Close the energetic loop/break the connection.

For the third step above, some schools of magick will have you make the "sign of Harpocrates" which is simply bringing a single index finger to your closed lips. I have found that stamping a foot, making a gesture with palms together, bowing, grunting, or a simple phrase such as "so mote it be" or some other ones of affirmation can be all effective. Use what works best for you after experimenting.

Exercise #41: Banishment by Word or Tone

Beforehand, choose a word or tone that you want to use. This could be something like the name of a rune, a simple phrase such as "go away", or just a high-pitched tone.

1. Cycle your energy. Focus on your intent to get rid of energy, and let that intent influence your personal energy. Cycle the chosen energy of banishment.
2. Release the word or tone towards your target. Adding a gesture may be effective to aid you (for example, holding outstretched closed hands up and pushing them forward like you are getting rid of something).
3. Break the energetic connection by making the sign of Harpocrates.

If this is done for an entire space, repeat for the four main directions at a minimum, and end up where you started while breaking the connection at each direction.

The goal with banishing with breath, tones, or words of power is more to disrupt and break apart the unwanted energies. Sound is an effective banishment tool. Some simple ways to use sound that are less "ceremonial" are to banish with screaming or laughter.

Exercise #42: Banishment by Sigil

1. Create a personal sigil for banishment using the "letter reduction method". This sigil should be something quick and easy to commit to memory. The example sigil (pictured) is from the word "AWAY" – using the A, W, and Y, and looks like an arrowhead. You can also use anything you feel is protective or aggressive – from pentacles to the sign for Mars, or anything similar.

2. Cycle your energy. Focus on your intent to get rid of energy, and let that intent influence your personal energy. Cycle the energy of banishment.

3. Draw the sigil in the air aggressively with the energy you have gathered, with the intent of that energy going away from you and your space. In the sigil above, I would recommend drawing the sigil with each line coming away from you and going out.

4. Stamp your foot in affirmation of breaking the energetic connection.

Exercise #43: Banishment by Tone and Gesture

1. Cycle your energy. Focus on your intent to get rid of energy, and let that intent influence your personal energy.

2. Create a mudra with both hands by joining your left and right thumbs, and your left and right index fingers, to make a triangle.

3. Place the mudra over your Third eye.
4. Make a tone, and then draw it out intensely out by making it louder and forcing more air out.
5. When the tone is as intense as you can make it, release the energy towards your target while forcefully making a gesture away from you with extending your arms and hands away from you.
6. Clasp your palms together and bow to break the energetic connection.

You can experiment with using gesture, sound, and sigil together. I have found that using them in combination creates layered and complex effects that are more effective through the combination. You this all the time in rituals like the "Lesser Banishing Ritual of the Pentagram". Find what works best for you in creating your own banishments as wells as what manner is most effective for you in breaking energetic connections at the end of the banishment.

Sometimes banishment is not about the large stuff. You might need to get rid of a small thing energetically and very quickly. I was doing work to remove a magickal "dart", a focused piece of energy thrown at someone to do them ill will, and once I removed it from their aura, I needed to put it someplace. I have found the following exercise useful for such things.

Exercise #44: Energetic Waste Disposal

1. Ground and keep grounding by visualizing the core at the center of the Earth and feeling its energetic effect on you.
2. Pull energy from the core of the Earth to a spot within arm's reach. You should be creating and maintaining a vertical access point of energy from the Earth to that spot. This can be done with visualization and gesture combined.
3. Mentally hold this vertical shaft of energy, feeling and visualizing it like a chute from where you are to the Earth's core.

4. Imagine a lid to this chute of energy and open it. With one hand.
5. With your other hand make a ball of energy, put as much negative emotion as you can into it.
6. Drop the ball of energy into the chute and close the lid.

With practice and familiarity, you should be able to summon and access the "chute" at any time. Conversely, you can simply feel the energy you are trying to banish, ground it out, and let it slip through your fingers almost like energetic "sand".

Warding

Warding a location is a way or protecting your space. Think of it as a permanent magick circle. This is useful when a space needs energetic connection or if you want to seal a space off for the reasons of protection, privacy, concealment, or camouflage. It is also a technique for marking your magickal territory to ward off disruptive forces. Many magickal practitioners will ward their entire home. This is very similar in theory to how we can manipulate our aura to make it more protective. Everything – living and non-living – has an aura and energy that can be manipulated.

Exercise #45: Warding a Room

1. Decide on a sigil of protection. This can be something you create or research (for example, runes).
2. Purify the space energetically.
3. Mark the edge of the space energetically, so that you are sending energy to the floor then raising it to the ceiling to make your one-dimensional line into a two-dimensional shape.
4. Visualize an energetic ceiling and roof.

5. Cycle your energy. Think of the energy you want to ward the room with (for example, protection, aggression, etc.) and cycle that energy through your body.
6. Draw the sigil in the four directions of the room (you could also have an individual sigil for each direction).
7. Go to the middle of the room and center.

Warding can also be done outside of a room or building. In that manner, the wards would almost be like a safe or a lockbox. I have found this to be an effective technique. When I use it, I often make an energetic keyhole, and make a key out of my personal energy to lock and unlock the wards.

Circle Casting

Prentis Hemphill once said that "Boundaries are the distance at which I can love you and me simultaneously". Similarly in magick, boundaries are the places that you can do magickal work and invite work with spiritual forces. Boundaries are important, and when a witch casts a magickal circle or energetic sphere, many schools of magick will say that you are creating a boundary between the mundane and magickal worlds or keeping negative forces out. This approach is useful when you are doing work that needs a more "sterile" magickal environment where you know what forces are being called and produced.

Casting a circle is like warding in terms of technique. You are creating an energetic seal, but the difference is that the three-dimensional energetic shape you make is temporary – it must be cast at the beginning of your spiritual work and taken down at the end. The phrase "casting a circle" is a bit of misnomer. You are really casting a sphere that is cut in half by the floor.

The "circles" you cast should leave enough room for you to function within. You can also cast a "circle" in any shape such as the platonic solids. The shape of your "circle" can influence your magick and help aid it. For example, casting a pyramid instead of a sphere would be useful in any spellwork for change or transformation. Once the energy is out there, it can also be manipulated with your mind. You could cast a sphere but change its shape once it is cast or you can make additions (for example, spikes on the outside for extra protection/warding).

Cosmology and Astrology

Sometimes I find it more useful to think that we are creating a space that reflects the Universe itself, instead of marking off psychic territory, and use a more holistic worldview. For the earth centered spiritualist, everything is sacred in many ways. Theologically speaking, the witch or Pagan typically looks at the Universe in a pantheistic worldview – this is the belief that spirit and matter, Heaven, and Earth, are all part of one whole thing. Pantheism usually comes up against the dualistic Judeo-Christian worldview that ranks Spirit over Earth. Dualistic worldviews can be dangerous since they put the world of ideas over the world of matter. This makes it easier to put a philosophy (especially an oppressive one) over the needs of the Earth, all living things, and individual human lives.

Pantheism, or the pantheistic mindset, calls us to view magick in terms of the magick circle as being the boundary and magickal focus of the personal universe, or microcosm. In this manner, the magickal practitioner re-creates the Universe, or macrocosm. Setting up sacred space illustrates the sacredness of all things and fills our space with something special and holy.

Every symbol set is a psychic map, or psychocosm, that is overlaid on the terrain of the Universe. To interact with the Universe in its rawest and most pure sense, is a mystical experience that is without words, but every metaphysical symbol set (for example, runes, tarot, numerology, astrology, etc.) seeks to describe what the Universe is.

A popular set of magickal correspondences that describe the Universe are the 12 signs of the zodiac. They are probably one of the most well known in the "non-magickal" world. The zodiac is literally the wheel of the year, with your sun sign (what people traditionally mean when they ask what your sign is) being when you were born in relation to the annual calendar. While we talk more about creating sacred space in the next chapter, we can talk about how sigils can help set that up. For now, please note that each zodiac symbol helps direct the energy of each zodiac sign.

To prepare for the next exercise, a brief astrological tutorial/ refresher is needed. Each zodiac sign has an element attached to it (for example, Taurus is an Earth sign). See the list below.

Aries (Fire) March 21 to April 20
Life force, will, ambition, energy

Taurus (Earth) April 21 to May 20
Loyalty, patience, practical, stable

Ⅱ

Gemini (Air) May 21 to June 21
Clever, Sociable, Talkative, Intelligent

Cancer (Water) June 22 to July 22
Protective, emotional, nurturing

Leo (Fire) July 23 to August 22
Expressive, Confident, Regal

𝕸

Virgo (Earth) Aug 23 to September 22
Organized, helpful, Idealistic

♎

Libra (Air) September 23 to October 22
Peace Loving, Diplomatic, Fair, Balanced

♏

Scorpio (Water) October 23 to November 21
Mysterious, Transformative, Daring

Sagittarius (Fire) November 22 to December 21
Honest, Passionate, Adventurous

Capricorn (Earth) December 22 to January 19
Conservative, Hard Working, Responsible

Aquarius (Air) January 20 to February 18
Unique, Creative, Original

Pisces (Water) February 19 to March 20
Empathic, Emotional, Mystical

Exercise #46: Creating the Zodiac Wheel

1. Memorize the symbols or have illustrations of them handy.
2. Ground, center, cycle your energy, and purify the room with energy.
3. Cast an energetic sphere.
4. Start in any direction, cast the sign of Aries. As you do so, project outwards into the sigil the energy of "ambition" and "will" from Aries.

5. Move around the circle a few steps and cast the next sign. Repeat until all the zodiac signs have been used in the circle.

6. Take time to meditate on what this energetic zodiac wheel feels like for some time.

7. Banish the zodiac energy by feeling for the sigils and either absorbing them, projecting a sense of gratitude, and thanking them, or drawing the sigils again and imagining that energy going back to where it came. Break the energetic connection at each sign.

8. Purify the space with energy and uncast the circle by grounding the energy out or absorbing it.

9. Center and reflect.

I like to purify the space I am using before and after any magickal work as a matter of etiquette. I do not like to leave an area energetically charged since I do not know how the leftover energies I gathered might influence or affect someone other than myself. Typically, I do not meditate after casting a circle like in the manner above, but I find it useful when using a different symbol set than the four elements to acquaint myself with the different energy and to take note of its effects for further magickal work.

Blessing

At this point, with practice and finding what works best for you personally, you should be able to banish energy from an area, purify the space, make an energetic three-dimensional magickal "working area", and call in any energy you need. The last aspect of creating sacred space is to add the energy that you specifically want to work with. You really have done this by invoking elements, astrological energy, etc., but if you want to further influence your circle you can also bless simply by focusing on a specific energy and letting it radiate. For example, if you wanted to focus on emotional magickal work, you would call the four elements, and then energetically fill the area with the energy of Water.

Some other ways to bless a space with a specific energy are:

1. Praying while imaging that energy radiating outward to the entire space.
2. Drawing a sigil in the middle of your space and imagine it getting big enough to fill the space.
3. Make a tone(s) that evokes the feelings of that energy.
4. A popular way blesses a space is to asperge the area with holy water. While this book covers how to do magick with energy primarily, sometimes it is useful to employ physical tools to add to the effectiveness of the magick.

Exercise #47: Holy Water

1. Get a glass of water that is has been purified physically (for example, distilled water).
2. Cycle and draw down the energy of Heaven/Spirit.
3. As you keep drawing it down, make a tone (this could be a high – or low-pitched hum) and draw energy into the water using your fingers to guide it from Heaven to the water.
4. Imaging the water glowing with energy.
5. Close off the energy by saying a word of affirmation (for example, "blessed be").
6. Use the water as you wish for purification of the space or an object.

You can actually taste the difference in the water, and I recommend a "before" and "after" taste.

Before we go to the next part on advanced magick and how to apply what was covered earlier for further applications, I would like to pause and thank you for coming on this journey so far. The next section will be even more interesting, but do not forget to attempt to master the basic before moving forward, and do not feel as if you cannot go back to cover something again.

Part II
Advanced Energy Work

Chapter 7

Advanced Energy Healing

Summary: Energy Healing Guidelines, Beyond Basic Energy Healing and Diagnosis, Chakra Healing, Sound Healing, Psychic Surgery, Boosting the Energetic Immune System, Physical Healing, Distance Healing, Ethics

Energy Healing Guidelines

I view energy healing very seriously. Manipulating your own energy is one thing but working with someone else's energy is a different matter. I think the best metaphor for energy work on another person is to think of it like going into an operating room. Everything needs to be sterile energetically – everything from the space you are in, to your personal energy, to the energy of any tools you may use. Before doing energy healing, the first things I like to do to prepare my personal energy are:

1. Meditation.
2. Purification.
3. Condense my aura.
4. Put on an energetic suit of armor to protect myself.

Meditation is to clear any wandering thoughts and intentions that might hinder the work. Thought shapes energy, so it is beneficial to clear any unnecessary ones and to get into a magickal headspace to do healing work. Meditation also helps to get into a relaxed (alpha) state that is the bare minimum, needed to do energy work effectively.

Purification of the self, and the space we operate in, is always necessary to do for ourselves and the places we operate in. We do not want to "infect" someone with the negative vibes, energies, or emotions of the places we do the healing work or from ourselves. We do not want to do more harm than good. I would say there are exceptions in some cases. For example, if you are doing healing work outdoors, you probably will not need to purify the space as much as you would need to set up sacred space.

Condensing the aura may seem like an odd thing to do, but it is to protect the practitioner and the healing recipient (since I am not a medical doctor, I do not feel right using the term "patient"). The technique is basically to be aware of the aura; see, feel, and imagine it shrinking almost to the skin, but not touching it; and maintain the effect by way of concentration, a trigger word, or anything else to remind you to keep the aura at the condensed level. A more condensed aura is also easier to manage.

Lastly, I always put on a protective energetic layer outside my aura. This energetic covering is designed to be disposed of. I summon energy that is protective, yet light, so that I do not feel weighted down by it (unless you are dealing with something extremely toxic then in that case, I might create an entire energetic "armor").

Beyond Basic Energy Healing and Diagnosis

Energy healing is dealing specifically with the astral body. The easiest way to heal this is to imagine the astral body as a body of white light and fill in any gaps with light you provide. The energy used is not your person energy, as this would be too depleting, but the energy used from cycling energy between Heaven and Earth. We can add extra power by diagnosing the energy problems and adding the appropriate and specific energy. On this theory, the more specific the energy, the greater the healing effect.

It is difficult to do any type of healing without knowing what the problem is and deciding on what energies to use can be challenging but is less so with proper diagnosis. A medical doctor might propose tests, x-rays, and any other method. Luckily, we have skills to detect energetic problems in terms of feeling energy and viewing it with second sight.

Beyond that we have the various mental maps and occult correspondences to guide our way. Most energetic issues or disease come from an imbalance of internal forces. If we overlay a correspondence map on the top of the experiences, we can see where things are and use the appropriate energy. I have talked a lot about chakras since they are system for dealing directly with the energetic body so I want to use that system as a basis for a lot of the healing work I do directly to the energetic body.

Chakra Healing

One metaphysical correspondence set that is valuable in our cases of imbalances is the theory of the chakras. We covered the basics of the chakra system earlier, and now let us look at the role they play in energetic health as the chakras are the major organs of our energetic bodies. Chakras are linked to our physical, emotional, mental, energetic, and spiritual health. What affects one aspect can affect them all.

The main problems that charkas develop are; they can become blocked, strained, have an excess of energy, or a deficiency of energy. Since chakra energy is flowing in and out, circulating, and being maintained – any problem with those essential functions will put the chakra out of its natural order and cause imbalances. These main issues are:

Blocked – The chakra energy is not flowing in and out or circulating and is stuck. This can occur when trauma to the mode of consciousness associated with the chakra occurs, or with physical damage to that area on the physical body.

Blockages can be signs that the chakra energy is repressed and that there is a pattern in terms of life habits, thoughts, or emotional coping mechanisms that need to be addressed. For example, a person who grew up in poverty might have a blocked root chakra until that trauma is addressed.

Strained – When a chakra is strained, barely any energy is used in the chakra. This can be the result of burn out, stress, or trauma. The chakra is retaining very little energy. A person who has loved someone very much and received nothing in return for many years may have a strained heart chakra.

Excess – Too much energy is expressed to the outside world. This occurs when too much is energy is given out and not enough taken back in. This might happen with a person that tries to please others too much – causing an excess in the sacral chakra.

Deficiency – Not enough energy and attention is given to the chakra or the mode of consciousness associated with it.

Chakra problems typically do not happen alone. It is uncommon for someone to have energetic issues in just one chakra. Someone may have problems with anxiety and there will be an excess of energy in their third chakra (will), while there may be a correlation between problems with the third eye (vision) being similarly overstimulated.

Diagnosing chakra issues is sometimes used with a pendulum, or even done with divination tools such as tarot. This can be done very easily, but sometimes a tool is not always handy. To diagnose basic chakra problems with only energy, you can feel the energy of the chakra in coordination with second sight. A blocked chakra's energy will flow horizontally and be in the shape more of a horizontal line. Strained chakras are the opposite and will usually flow vertically. Excess chakras will have too much energy moving often too quickly. Deficient chakras may be shrunk or weak. The main things to pay attention to are the movement of the energy and its intensity. Below are some of the descriptions of chakra issues mostly as they pertain to thoughts and emotions. While these problems may eventually manifest in physical symptoms, hopefully they can be resolved before they get to that point. Below is a summary of health and problems as they pertain to each chakra.

Root – A balanced and open root chakra helps someone be grounded and healthy. As the root is the place of getting physical needs met, someone that expressed these qualities should have a healthy first chakra. Blocked root chakra behavior would be someone that is needy – trying to find someone to ground them to life when they cannot do so themselves. Fear is the province of an unhealthy root and may be exhibited across the board with any energetic imbalances here. Strained root chakras may make a person fatigued or weary – draining someone of their vital energies. Excessive root chakra energies are things you might see in dictators or tyrants as an overabundance of this energy may cause tendencies towards being a bully or self-centeredness. Deficiencies in the root may be linked with low self-esteem.

Sacral – A healthy sacral chakra is associated with being creative, emotionally balanced, and friendly. As this is often the "sex chakra", this would include a healthy sex life and a strong, yet balanced sense of sexuality. A blocked sacral chakra may be linked with feelings of guilt or shame. There are extremes with a blocked sacral chakra – someone may over-sensitive on one hand, or unexpressive and standoffish on the other. Strained second chakra energy may be related to poor boundaries. Excessive sacral chakra behavior would be associated with sex addiction, unbalanced emotions, or emotional manipulation. Deficient sacral chakras can correlate with an unfriendly or cold manner.

Solar Plexus – The solar plexus chakra is the seat of pure willpower. A person with a balanced one will exhibit a strong work ethic, be centered in their personal power, and have warm and perhaps playful personality traits. A blocked chakra could influence someone to be fearful, timid, and avoid any new things. Strained solar plexus behavior would influence someone to be flighty and unreliable. Excess solar plexus chakra energy can make someone aggressive, angry, and controlling. While a balanced person, in regard to this chakra, would have a healthy work ethic – an excess would cause a tendency towards being a workaholic who puts work above all else. In contrast to the excess, deficient chakra behavior would be passive. There would also be a tendency towards low self-esteem and self-worth.

Heart – The heart is the middle of the chakra system, and as such balances the higher and lower chakras. A healthy heart chakra leads someone to be compassionate, loving, and nurturing. Blocked heart energy is that of self-pitying and self-loathing; a person that would have problems loving themselves and receiving love. Strained heart chakra people are typically people pleasers who pour love out of themselves and not give enough to themselves. Excessive heart energy can be smothering – leading someone to be possessive, jealous, and co-dependent. When heart chakra energy is deficient, it leads people towards isolation and depression.

Throat – The throat chakra is the seat of clear communication, so healthy energy here is that of clear communication and outward creative expression of the self. On the other hand, blocked chakra energy may be an indication of issues communicating clearly, or at all, and have problems expressing themselves. Issues with telling the truth and difficulty finding words may relate to a strained throat chakra. Excess throat energy might be connected to someone who is arrogant and self-righteous – as if their words mean more than anyone else's – or someone that speaks too much without thinking. Deficient throat energy may indicate a fear of speaking aloud or a general difficulty in putting thoughts and feelings into words.

Third Eye – The healthy third eye is the home of intuition, imagination, and perception. A blocked third eye can lead someone to delusions, while a strained one may lead a person to being misled by others or have issues with understanding reality. An excess of third eye energy may make someone too logical and over analytical. Deficient third eye energies may indicate a person that is forgetful or lacks imagination.

Crown – The crown chakra that is balanced and healthy offers the gifts of thoughtfulness, peace, and understanding. This is the place of blossoming and full spirituality. Blocked, the crown chakra can be linked with intolerance and indecisiveness. A strained crown chakra may cause confusion. In excess, crown energy can be manic or lead to traits such as megalomania or over-intellectualism. When the crown energy is deficient, a person may exhibit extreme cynicism or have rigid beliefs.

In action, it is wise to have something nearby to write down the diagnosis. I like to start analyzing a person's chakra in order from top to bottom. After looking at the entire energetic chakra reading, I will ask the healing recipient questions to verify if they are having issues. For example, someone with an excess of the solar plexus chakra may have stomach issues and insomnia. After each chakra state is verified, then we need to see if there is a pattern. The next exercise works best if there are two people, and each person is taking turns diagnosing the other, but can also be done by yourself.

Exercise #48: Chakra Diagnosis

1. Get something to take notes on each chakra.
2. Lay the healing recipient down on their back, or alternatively lay down if by yourself.
3. Go through each chakra, starting at the root. Use second sight and use your receptive hand to feel the energy. Determine if each chakra is balanced, blocked, strained, or in excess or deficiency. You can use the chart at the bottom as an example. Diagnose through feeling the energy and seeing it through the body using 2nd sight.
4. Ask the healing recipient, or yourself, if there are any corresponding behaviors or factors that coincide with the specific findings.
5. See if there is a relationship between similar energetic patterns.
6. Make note of the patterns.

Chakra/ Location/ Number	Normal	Blocked	Strained	Excess	Deficient
Root/1st					
Sacral/ Navel/2nd					
Solar Plexus/3rd					
Heart/4th					
Throat/5th					
Third Eye/6th					
Crown/7th					

Once you know what is going on, then comes the work of restoring the chakra. I think of chakra energy in terms of a spiritual force that exists both within us and outside of us. When I am healing a chakra, I am drawing on that outside, archetypical chakra energy from Spirit to balance and set things right. The technique I find the most useful is the following:

1. Cycle energy from the Heavens, and concentrate on that chakra force in its pure, healed form.
2. Send that energy to the healing recipient directly into that chakra.
3. If there is a problem with how it circulates, retains, or expresses energy or out, use your hands to move the energy to where it should (remember energy follows attention, so using your hands is optional). For example, with a blocked chakra – the energy needs to be manipulated so that it is flowing in and out while circulating.
4. Check the energy afterwards to make sure it is restored, balanced, and healthy. Repeat healing as necessary.
5. Afterwards, talk about the behaviors and life patterns that affected the energy. A good healing will help reset someone and give them the energy they need to make the lifestyle changes necessary that coordinate with the healthy energetic flow.

Effective chakra healing is that combination of fixing energetic flow, while infusing it with healthy chakra energy in what is basically an energetic transfusion. If there is too little energy, I draw it from Heaven, too much – then I ground it to Earth. Energetic healing will sometime have to be repeated if the healing recipient was not able to take the "reset" as an opportunity to heal their lives, but this should not be an opportunity for judgement, but for compassion instead.

Sound Healing

As we say in the first section of the book, words of power or tones can be effective in moving energy. An effective, yet simple, method is to use sound to heal the chakras. Many practitioners have a scale that they have used to great effect. See the below chart for a standard set of notes and tones to use in sound healing. Using notes are especially helpful when you have instruments or tuning forks handy. I prefer using tones since I can feel the sound resonate in my body, and the connection I have feeling that resonance between our energies is useful in feeling if healing is happening. Typically speaking higher tones are used to heal the upper chakras, and lower tones for the lower ones.

Chakra Location	No.	Note	Tone
Root	1st	C	Urrrr
Sacral Navel	2nd	D	Oooo
Solar Plexus	3rd	E	Ohhhh
Heart	4th	F	Ahhhh
Throat	5th	G	Ayyyy
Third Eye	6th	A	Eyyye
Crown	7th	B	Eeeee

I have found the above reference helpful, and I have found that everyone is different. My trick is to experiment with finding the right tone for the right situation and energetic circumstance. When you find the right tone, repeat it as many times as necessary until the chakra intuitively feels right and starts to energetically "lock" back into a healthy state. I have used tuning forks, and tones with my mouth, to do this in practice. You will know you have the right tone when you feel a resonance between what is making the tone and the part of the energetic system you are healing. Experiment making tones, ranging from high pitches to low hums, and see how they interact with your chakras before using this tool on others. When I use these tones on myself, I find it is a great way to balance

Psychic Surgery

Energy is everywhere, and it can affect and infect us in subtle ways. Sometimes negative energy comes at us from other magickal practitioners, or even "normal" people, to places and objects. This negative, or unwanted, energy may disrupt our moods, thoughts, and physical health – leaving us with fatigue, and intense unwanted emotions. I have removed anything from energetic objects implanted into someone maliciously, to parasites (semi-sentient entities created through intense emotion that are as aware as any physical parasite), and even energetic viruses (negative energy signatures passed from person to person).

Some parasites are mostly benign, like an energetic tapeworm – others are more damaging. There is one class of parasite that is common. It causes sensitivity to sunlight, and intense emotions. It is scorpion or spider-like and will attach to the spine. Psychic surgery is the swiftest cure to it, while opening a portal to solar energy to direct on the person you are doing healing for.

When more invasive work is needed when energy cannot be purified or grounded out. Psychic surgery can be employed when there are either manifested or put into someone's energy. The procedure is as follows:

1. Diagnose the healing recipient's energy. When scanning the aura, or energetic body, pay attention to any dark spots that seem more "solid" than anything else around it.
2. Make an incision in the outer aura using an energetic knife to get to the afflicted area.

3. Find the energy to be removed and grasp it by its outer aura. Dispose of the energy.
4. Energetically seal the healing recipient back up.
5. Purify any energies as needed.

Going back to chakras – sometimes setting a chakra is not effective, or there are more deep-rooted issues. Sometimes a chakra needs to be given a boost. In this case, there is chakra replacement. In chakra replacement, the following technique is employed:

1. Diagnose the chakra and attempt balancing and healing the chakra. If this fails, consider replacement therapy.
2. Make an incision in the aura using an energetic knife to get to the afflicted area.
3. Gently grasp the chakra energy and dispose of it carefully.
4. Purify the energetic wound.
5. Create a ball of archetypical chakra energy. Fashion it to the appropriate size, and gently connect it to the healing recipient.
6. Make sure the chakra is connected to the spine of the healing recipient.
7. Restore energetic flow by restoring the elemental functions of each chakra. Make sure it is connected to the other chakras.
8. Energetically seal the healing recipient back up.
9. Purify any energies as needed.

Chakra surgery should be one of the last resorts if you cannot heal the chakra by normal means. I do not recommend using your own chakra energy to create a new chakra for someone. They may inherit any issues, character traits, habits, or trauma that you carry within them. Psychic surgery can and should be used in coordination with mundane tools such as therapy.

Boosting the Energetic Immune System

When someone is the victim of things such as an energetic parasite, it can sometimes happen for the same reason as physical illnesses occur in that the immune system is down. Magickly speaking, this would coincide with poor energetic health in terms of not maintaining the aura, chakras, personal shields, etc. I like to take a "solar bath" by casting a circle and invoke the sun by drawing the planetary sigil for the sun at four corners or above me. Drawing energy into yourself through cycling with Heaven and Earth or invoking energies that you find empowering are a great way to stay strong and energetically healthy.

Physical Healing

Aiding physical healing is possible with energy work. With every physical part of the body, there is an energetic double. By healing the energy that corresponds to the physical, you can aid in the healing of the body – making injuries heal faster, and sometimes making any lasting damage less severe.

The best technique is to see and feel the energy that needs to be healed and fill it in with similar energy that is around the "wound" and eliminating the "energetic double" of the physical ailment. Sometimes the results can be dramatic, and sometimes all you can do is energetically aid medical cures that are already being used.

The way to make physical healing work more effective, and really any energy work, is for the practitioner to be in as deep as trance as possible. This requires the practitioner to get into as deep a meditation state as possible. If possible, it is excellent if you can get the healing recipient into as deep a trance or meditative state as possible. For example, if you can lead a healing recipient in a guided meditation where they see the energetic damage with you and see it being healed as you do the work.

Distance Healing

We cannot always be near the person we want to heal. Energy is everywhere and can be anywhere. To do distance healing, we can go about it a few of different ways.

Use astral projection to be in the same location as the person being healed and send and coordinate healing energies from there. I will typically be in contact with the person I am healing via phone or text to verify that they feel me there. I will also tap them on the shoulder energetically and ask them if they feel it and at which shoulder to verify, I am projecting properly.

Make a sigil specific to the situation and use the sigil as a portal to send energy. This has the extra effect of shaping the energy to your specific need. I will use the reduction method to make a sigil as outlined above. An example of a statement of intent to start the sigil work would be "It is my will that Steve be healed of his migraine". I would have the unique letters of I T S M Y W L H A E V B D O F G R N that could be made into a sigil and a word of power that can be chanted while sending healing energy.

You can also use evocation to summon the person's astral body to you and do healing on that person's energetic body directly. You can use a standard evocation ritual as outlined in a later chapter.

Ethics

I am putting ethics here as my disclaimer. I feel like it goes without saying that you should not heal someone or mess with their energy without their permission, but there is always that one person that will complain that I did not tell them. Also, please follow basic morality. If you need a guide, please go by the "platinum rule" which is "treat others the way they want to be treated". If after all consideration, you are not completely sure that what you are doing is right or ethically sound, consider doing a divinatory reading, or just not doing it at all.

Since everything is energy, and we all draw from the same giant Universal pool of energy, whatever changes we make or intention we put out there is bound to affect us. Use caution when deciding on a course of action, and meditate upon what your energy will affect.

Chapter 8

Cord Cutting

Summary: What Are Cords? On Energetic Bodies and Cords, Discovering Cords, Elements of Connection, Mental and Emotional Analysis, Types of Cords, Chakras and Cords, Cord Cutting Process, Healing the Wound, Aftercare, Other Uses of Cord Cutting

Cord cutting is a sub-section of psychic surgery. Many times, when people talk about cord cutting it is along the lines of "I had a bad breakup, I really need to cut my ties and connection to them." Usually this is a sort of cathartic way to bring closure to a relationship and start things new. While this is not always the case, I find that most people are suffering from energetic connections to previous relationships, places, and events from the past that we no longer have a current relationship with. We can be constantly connected to "dead" relationships that are weighing us down energetically, mentally, emotionally, and sometimes physically.

What Are Cords?

Before we get into cord cutting itself, we need to look at what the cords are and explore our own. To put it simply, cords are energetic connections. The root of these cords is you, and more specifically your energetic body. Everything is connected, and connections that are meaningful manifest in the energetic body as cords – lines of energy that bind us to another person, place, thing, or event. Typical cord cutting consists of two to three main parts:

1. Sympathetic Magick – This is the basic cord cutting ritual when people think of cord cutting where two candles are

placed across from each other with a cord, thread, or piece of string connecting them. One candle represents you, and the other the person that you are cutting ties with. The candles are burnt symbolically until they have completely run out. I have found that this step is optional, and at the same time physical representations can be helpful.

2. Energetic Cord Cutting – This is cord cutting of the actual energy that connects two people/entities. This can be done without the candle ritual but should be done in conjunction with it.

3. Aftercare & Healing – Emotional care after ritual and/or cord cutting. Healing work should also be done where the cords are connected to the energetic body.

I have found that using the physical tools for cord cutting are not necessary, but like anything in this book, the energetic can be used with the physical. You can use candles connected with a cord in conjunction with energetic cord cutting. The process would be to get two candles signifying you and what you are cutting the cord from, tie a piece of thread between both, and light both candles. Use basic fire safety and prevention. In my experience, the candle process is far more effective when coupling it with energetic cord cutting.

On Energetic Bodies and Cords

Our energetic bodies are where emotions are stored. When we have a physical interaction with something, our emotional bodies make a record of it. For example, if someone goes into a room where an argument takes place, even people that are not metaphysically inclined will feel something is off about that place. This is because the energy of that place has been changed due to keeping energetic "recordings" of what happened there. In a similar way, we are shaped by the energies of what happens to us and where we go. This is not enough to create an energetic cord. Most of the ways that we are affected by energy can be transformed into something else through purification, ritual, meditation, or other means. Our energetic bodies are fluid. We will go into the process of how a cord is created.

The mind is a powerful tool. The mental body, like the physical and the energetic, play a role in how cords are formed. The language of the mental body is through symbols, archetypes, and language. When someone says the word "chair", another person might think of the chair they are personally sitting in or a chair from childhood. When someone says the name of someone you have strong emotions for, images, words, and memories may flood your consciousness. The mental body stores the data from language and conscious memory. This contrasts with the unconscious, direct, and more visceral information of the energetic body. While we cannot simply draw a memory out of our heads easily (although therapy can help over time), we can manipulate the emotions attached to those memories by directly manipulating our energetic bodies.

Discovering Cords

Now that we are familiar with seeing and feeling energy, we can start feeling the cords that we are dealing with directly. Now that you can feel and see the energy that cords are made of, you are closer to the process of dealing with them. We will explore specific types of cords as they relate to the energetic body later, but for now focus on your ability to sense them. Some people are more focused on one sense than another. It is best to try to see and feel the cords, but if you can only do one and not the other, you will still be able to release the cords you need to.

Exercise #49: Discovering Your Cords

1. Using what we learned from the previous exercises, we will use our sense of energetic touch and second sight to discover our cords.

2. Rub your hands together to get them sensitive to sensing energy or do Exercise #2 again.

3. Extend your most sensitive hand from 1 to 2 feet horizontally and vertically above your head.

4. Slowly lower your hand and feel for any area where energy collects. You might feel this as a warm or cool feeling, a tingle that is almost electric, or a tension in the air.
   When you find an energetic spot, move your fingers horizontally and run your fingers along this length. Test to see if this is a cord by tapping it slowly. If it is a cord, you may feel anything from a buzz to discomfort.

5. Continue exploring the cords of your body from your head to the base of your spine.

6. Repeat, and this time try to see the cords with your "second sight" as you feel them.
   Cords typically form in the area from your head to the base of your spine, with major correlations to the major chakras. I have found that cords are generally connected with them, and it helps to look at cords through the perspective of the chakra system to "untie" and "unwind" cords.

7. There is almost never just one cord when doing a cord cutting. Connections are built over time and usually based on various parts of our lives. For example, it would be very difficult to do a complete cord cutting for an ex-spouse if you are still raising children together. In this case, you would cut the cords that represent your romantic relationship, but not the one(s) that connect you to your ex via your shared relationship with your children.

Elements of Connection

Before we start cutting cords, it is useful to understand how the cords are created in the first place. Cord creation, and really any connection, goes through a four-part elemental process.

This process was discovered through countless case studies and attempts to deconstruct how connection happens. We can argue everything can be broken down into creative processes. The "elements of connection" just break down how we connect and join socially and energetically.

Foundation (Earth) – When two people connect for the first time, it is usually not out of nothing. Typically speaking there is a connection made by virtue of something common. This can be as simple as being at the same event, or as complex to having multiple areas of interest. For example, people at a convention will often form strong bonds since they are at a gathering of people that share their similar hobbies and disposition. The more that one common thread (pun intended) is found, then typically the interactions that follow will reveal more things in common. The collection of these shared commonalities is the foundation for further opening. Some common foundations might be race, religion, belief systems, likes and dislikes, and if you are related by blood. I remember when I was in high school and one of the first questions, I would ask someone would be about what music they listened to. When we first meet people, we compare who we are with who they are in an effort to see if they are an ok person to connect with and if they are safe. Energetically speaking, we are establishing if it is alright to let down our shields and let their energy connect with ours.

Dynamic (Air) – Once several commonalities have been found, there is an excitement to finding someone with similar interests. This sense of excited energy moving back and forth between two subjects creates an energetic dynamic. In an ideal and healthy situation this dynamic energy flow is a fun, creative, and enriching process. Much of the dynamic is along the lines of what has been discovered in the "getting to know you" process of foundation, but it can also be about creating and sharing new experiences that are fun and exciting. In an unhealthy manner – dynamics of abuse will create a hurtful flow of energy that creates a foundation of trauma where more and more energy can be shared, taken, or malformed. In terms of our energetic bodies, this is when we open the personal bubbles of our field and share energy back and forth.

Charisma (Fire) – This is where foundations and dynamics reach a critical point. When there are enough connections and a strong enough dynamic, what one person/subject does will have as much influence as something the other would do. This is where when one person gets excited or is excited, then the other person will as well. This where personal boundaries break down due to the number of connections formed. The emotional energy of one person will cause us to feel what they feel.

Trust (Water) – Trust is the ultimate breakdown of two things into one. When a newborn baby cries, there is a phenomenon where other babies, that are nearby and can hear the sound and will start crying as well. This is called emotional contagion and is a healthy sign of development and empathy. This same process works when we are much older when we have let our guard down and the natural empathy that people develop in a healthy manner is devoted and focused on the relationship that is developing. There is plenty of a shared foundation, a strong flow of energy back and forth, and times where one person's emotions are superseded by another's. This is the place where two people almost seem to become one and what many people think of as the height of romantic love. Trust is where someone is most vulnerable, and on an energetic level is a free exchange of energy between all your energy centers without limit. Sometimes these feelings of openness are fleeting and come in bursts, but they can come in intense waves as well. Unhealthy aspects of this are when someone is too trusting or gets lost in the other person. Energetically speaking, it may be difficult to see where one person ends and another begins.

Sometimes connections are one way and exist mostly within a person. In this case the dynamic is of a person giving their energy away to something that cannot return it. Energy cycles back and forth, ebbing and flowing like the tides, but energy that is not cycling back can be a mental, emotional, and sometimes physical drain.

The above process is a way to diagram how connections, and thus cords, are formed. This is a typical process, but it may occur out of order. It might also happen between a place or thing, instead of a person. In this case, when the subject of the connection is not living in the traditional sense but has its own energy, the foundation is based more on the external world being a mirror for something inside the person; the dynamic would be based on how the person feels; the charisma and charm of the place sparking new feelings, and trust being established in the sense of an open and expansive love.

After this process occurs, the energetic results are the energetic cords. Based on how long the relationship lasts, and the work being put into it, the process of the "elements of connection" may repeat to form more cords or strengthen the ones that are present. Without energy being put into the connection, it may very fade over time. This is a natural process and happens in coordination with the normal life cycle of any relationship.

There are exceptions to the "elements of connection", sometimes we can connect very quickly with strangers. Have you ever seen someone in a crowd and felt an intense connection for just a few moments? Have you been helped by someone you didn't know and there was an instant chemistry? While these "instant cords" happen briefly and rarely, it does not mean that a cord is not formed that needs to be dealt with.

Cords are created through forming relationships, and our primary way of looking at the types of cords is in relation to the seven major chakras. Cord cutting is not just a magickal tool to end a painful or troubling connection or relationship. It is a way to purify oneself from things that are holding us back from our potential and drain our very life essence that we need to function every day in a healthy manner and have the mental and emotional space to do new things, grow emotionally, and evolve spiritually. It is wise to not just leap into cutting cords, but to understand and get to know them first. We can do this mentally and emotionally. The mind is the gateway to the emotions, and the emotions are the key that unlocks our spiritual energy.

Mental and Emotional Analysis

To make cord cutting as effective as possible, change must happen on an emotional, mental, and spiritual level. To create that change, we cannot just make it happen instantaneously – we need to do the work. Some cord cuttings are not effective because enough work is not put into it. This, and the next chapters, break down the "work" so that when we do the actual cord cutting it will be as powerful and permanent as possible. This speaks to the fact that sometimes what you put into spiritual work is what you get out of it.

To help analyze the effects of the cords on your life, I have created a brief questionnaire. The purpose is to help you think about your connections, and what cord(s) you may want to deal with.

Exercise #50: Cord Questionnaire

Please answer the following questions as honestly and completely as possible. I recommend writing them out, as opposed to answering them after the text like a workbook so that you can reuse the questionnaire at a later time when needed.

The subject(s) of the answer of your questionnaire can vary. This might be a person such as a romantic partner, a parent, friend, co-worker, or any person you connected with; a place such as a home from childhood or the place painful memories occurred; or even an event such as a traumatic incident or even major life milestones.

The Past

What are people, places, or things from the past that you feel still affect you?

Do you have any past relationships you feel that are unresolved? If so, who or what were they with?

How old were you and where were you at in life?

How did they begin? How did you feel at the beginning of the relationship?

How did those relationships end? How did you feel at the end of the relationship?

How did the relationship change who you are?

Do you have any regrets about the relationship? Do you wish it never happened?

What did you like or dislike about the person you were in relationship with?

The Present

Reflecting on the relationships from the last section, how do those relationships affect you now?

How do you feel physically when thinking about these past relationships?

How much time do you spend focusing on the past?

Do you feel that all relationships will be like your past ones?

Do you have intrusive or obsessive thoughts about the past that interrupt your daily life?

Do you feel that you have less energy now than you did in the past?

How do the relationships of the past make you feel about yourself?

The Future

If you had more energy, what would you use it for?

How would the future look if you were free from the pain or effects of your past?

What relationships could you explore if you had the time, energy, and emotional resources?

Now that we have used our mental processes to open ourselves up and stir up how we feel about the subjects of our cords, we can do some more work on feeling those emotions. This may also serve as work to do right before cutting the cords so that the actual cutting is cathartic, but not overwhelming.

Exercise #51: Emotional Waterfall

Since emotions are like water, and correspond as such in Western metaphysics, this exercise connects with elemental/Universal water to help break your emotions open enough to do the work of cord cutting. This can be very overwhelming, so please have an action plan ready for after-care, what do you need to feel happy and safe, and perhaps even have people on standby to talk to.

1. With your eyes open or closed, begin breathing in and out. Let your breathing become slow and labored.
2. Imagine that a waterfall of white light is descending upon you. It is a warm comforting light that allows you to feel safe. Breathing in safety and feeling warmth as you exhale.

3. Pay attention to any place in your body that is uncomfortable, especially places of tension, feelings in the chest or belly, or even physical pain.
   Breathe in and out paying attention to any discomfort or pain, say the first words that come to you.

4. As you say the words that come to you, feel the emotions behind them.
   Allow the emotions to flow off of you and from you into the waterfall and flow into the Earth.

5. Focus back on your breathing. Let the energies subside and open your eyes if they are closed when you are ready.

6. If you did not feel anything during this exercise, that is fine. Repeat as necessary. Emotions are not easy things to process or deal with. You may have had the words come to you without the emotion behind them, and that is ok. The goal is to feel and really be in those emotions so that you can cut the cord fully and not leave any remnants. This is why some cord cuttings may need to be repeated.

The emotions that you were able to feel, have a lot of energy, and much of that may be tied up in the cord you want to cut. We often take stress into our bodies and tense a certain way that we become stuck in. Cutting the cord will release the energy that you have stored up mentally, emotionally, and psychically.

Connections are very tied into emotions. Most of what gets some people in trouble are personal dynamics that are fueled by emotions and navigating these connections can be stressful. Some of this is miscommunication, of course, but other times another person's emotions can make us uncomfortable, and we need to put personal boundaries in place. Other times, we learn things about people and find that we want to disentangle ourselves more but cannot. This causes pain and frustration.

Types of Cords

There are few types of cords we should address before we go any further. Below are a few common types of cords to act as a guide to the types of cords you may find in your personal explorations of your energy or in that of people you may help.

Relationship – The most common kind of cord. These can range in location from the seven major chakras but can originate from any part of the body to another person. These cords are typically in groups, but it is possible to have just one cord connecting you to another person. This is especially true if it has been some time since the relationship ended. Relationship cords anchor you to another person and distribute energy freely between people based on the frequency and quality of energy that is pushed back and forth between them.

Location – These cords connect you to places. They function kind of like energetic roots to ground you in the energies of a specific location. They originate from the base of the spine typically, and usually branch out and are shaped like tree roots.

Memory – These cords may originate from the head and trail off into the air. These are cords that link you to energies of the past, but not necessarily connected to a person. They exist partially here and partially in other spiritual dimensions – mostly the astral. These cords are typically thinner than "relationship" and "place" cords.

Self-Cords – These are cords that connect us to aspects of ourselves. These are typically found internally but can be felt in meditation when someone is focused on their relationship with themself. When externalized, they often fold back onto themselves. There is a specific type of shadow work where you can externalize a fragment of your consciousness to deal with it – for example, a bad habit – then you would cut the cords with that aspect and reabsorb the energy.

Object Cords – These are cords that connect us to specific objects. They can be useful when trying to find lost objects – since you can focus on your connection to the object and feel the cord – but the strength of the cord is based upon how much emotion or energy you have put into the object. The other side is that sometimes we connect to mementos from the past and a cord cutting is needed to move on. These often originate from the hands but can form from any part of the body.

Exercise #52: Holding Cords

Holding the cords is part of the cord cutting process. You cannot cut something that you are not familiar with, and it is best that you understand it as intimately as possible. Energy follows attention, and the more you focus on the cord, the more it comes alive, and you can deal with it more effectively in cord cutting.

1. Open your hand chakras.
2. Feel around for a cord and pick a specific one. It does not matter the location, but it is best to pick the one that feels like it has the most energy. Relationship cords are usually the "heaviest".
3. You will feel the top of the cord first, if you are starting from the head down to feel the cord, but instead of just touching it, cup your hand around it with your fingers at the top of the cord and your thumb on the bottom.
4. Breathe in and out, until your breathing is slow, relaxed, and labored.

5. Feel the energy of the cord you are holding if you need to hold the cord with both hands.

6. Explore the cord by asking yourself the following questions, or ones that are similar: What does it feel like? Is it heavy or light? When you close your eyes and use second sight, are there colors? Do any images come to you? What emotions are you feeling? How does your body feel where the cord is connected?

7. If they are not already, close your eyes and focus on just the emotions of the cord. Let them flow in and out naturally. Try to name the emotions if you can.

8. When you are done exploring, bring your awareness to your body and your current state of being. Release the cord from your hand(s) and release the emotions from that connection. If necessary, do the emotional waterfall exercise and/or center and ground.

Chakras and Cords

Earlier, we talked about the major chakras. Let us explore the relationship between the cords and chakras more. The below chart is a way to see what type of cords are created as they relate to the chakras. The chakras are not just where the cord forms from, but it determines the type of cord. Below is a list to how the chakras and cords relate.

Chakra	Types of Cords
Root/Survival	Money, Bills, Food
Sacral Navel	Sex, Friendship, Social Relationships
Solar Plexus	Work, Partnership, Responsibilities
Heart	Love, Betrayal, Hate
Throat	Hobbies, Projects, Similar Interests
Third Eye	Long Term Goals, Point of View, Thoughts
Crown	Religion, Spirituality

Root – Since the root chakra is the energy center of survival and base needs, it is very much the foundation of who we are. Without getting our physical needs met, we cannot get the needs of social interaction, cultivating personal power, love, creativity, and spiritual expression met at all. When we live with people and share resources, we share a bond. In a family that lives together, the bond is even more intense and events such as preparing meals, sharing monetary resources, doing house chores only make it more so. Cords from the root chakra are based upon who we meet our needs for survival with.

Sacral – The sacral chakra is the center of emotions, sexuality, and social connections. This is probably one of the most active chakras in terms of creating cords. These are cords that are created through being in the same social sphere as another person – these are the cords of the tribe or group you are a part of. Sex obviously bonds you with another person by its intrinsic intimacy and sharing of the emotions and the senses. While sex for procreation is typically in the root chakra, sex for pleasure and fun concerns the sacral chakra. When someone has sex with another person, or shares sexual energy, there will typically be cords between the people involved. Since the sacral chakra is also a main emotional center, anyone, or anything we have strong emotions about may have cords that originate from here.

Solar Plexus – The solar plexus, or "will" chakra, is the place of personal power. Cords created with this energy center are usually those of shared responsibilities, work, and partnership. While root chakra work connections are typically about survival, 3rd chakra cords are more concerned with sharing power and exercising it in unison. Soldiers on a battlefield, co-workers in the same department, and people that partner together to accomplish any task would be bound by solar plexus cords. Solar plexus cords can also be created between a person and objects they work with or create.

Heart – The heart is the center of love. Anyone we love can have their cord originate from here. The cord connections can be like the 2nd chakra, but more intense, expansive, and developed. Love can be that for a romantic partner, a friend, parent or parent figure, love for all beings, or most importantly self-love. When love goes wrong, all the positive feelings do not go away all the time and can often transform into the opposite of hate. This is also the place where cords of betrayal can be found.

Throat – the throat chakra deals with how and what we communicate to others. A throat chakra cord may form when we find people with similar communication styles, expressions of self, or that we just find it easy to talk to. Everything from our clothing, how we speak, hobbies, and similarities of expression, may foster throat chakra connections.

Third Eye – The third eye is the chakra of insights – both mythical and otherwise. Going back to the "elements of connection", when we have a shared foundation, connection can happen. Having the same opinions, thoughts, and point of view are quick connections that can happen quickly. Since the third eye is the center of visualization, when we envision a future with someone, we create cords that come from here.

Crown – The crown chakra connects us to the Divine. As such, if we do spiritual work with someone, we form cords that originate here. Connections may be with people that share our religion and spiritual expressions. Cutting cords at the crown level must be done with some thought and consideration. We are all connected, and everyone and everything is connected in some manner. Use intuition in deciding if connections here need to be cut.

The aspects of life that each chakra corresponds to is directly related to what the cord's energy is. Let us say that I lived with a romantic partner for some time, thought we were soul mates, lived together, and eventually parted. My cord connecting them would include strands from the root chakra (since we lived together and helped each other through our basic needs), sacral and heart (since it was a romantic and sexual relationship), and even the Third Eye (due to using our imaginations to think of what our lives would be like forever). Some relationships are so strong that we throw our entire beings into them and most of the chakras would be involved since that connection occurred in many different fields of life experience that the chakras rule. By using the chakras as our shared metaphysical language, we can categorize the cords and better understand them. The more we understand them, the easier it is to cut the cords and enact lasting change.

Cord Cutting Process

While you can do the process of cord cutting rather quickly, it functions best when there is preparation. The more work you put into preparing for it, the longer lasting and more complete the changes will be. The basic process is below.

1. Set Intention.
2. Meditation.
3. Connecting with Cord.
4. Feeling the Emotions.
5. Cutting the Cord.
6. Healing Wound.
7. Ground & Center, Meditation, or After Care.

Setting the intention provides focus for the work. Meditation gets you into trance to have a greater effect. Connecting with the cord and feeling the emotions allow you to access the energy you are cutting.

For the actual cutting of the cord, you have a few options:

1. Cutting the Cord – You can cut the cord with an energetic tool in one hand – making a knife or forming the edge of your finger's aura into one. You can push the other end of the cord away from yourself., banish it, "burn" it energetically, ask for spiritual assistance, or use any other method that feels right.

2. Untangling the Cord – You may find that there is an energetic knot tying you to another person or a tangle of cords. If that is the case, you can untie the knot or untangle the cords with your command, intention, and visualization. If you are having problems with this, you can always cut the cord traditionally.

3. Pulling the Cord – It is possible to hold on to the cord firmly energetically and pull the cord from you. This is especially useful in circumstances where someone is taking your energy without your permission.

You may find that instead of cutting all the cords, you may want to keep some of them. This is useful if your relationship with the person has changed, and you do not need to banish them from your life completely.

Exercise #53 – Cutting the Cords
1. Decide on why you are cutting cords beforehand.

2. Sit in meditation until you are as relaxed as possible and starting at either your root or crown chakra, feel the first cord you want to cut.
3. Sit with the emotion of that cord while holding the cord with one hand.
4. With your other hand, visualize an energetic knife – or visualize the aura of your finger as ones – and cut the cord. Alternatively, you can, pull, untangle, or untie the cord.
5. Let go of your end of the cord and push away or banish the other end.
6. Retract or dispose of any energetic cutting tools.
7. Heal the wound energetically.
8. Rest and provide any aftercare you may need.

Healing the Wound

Healing the energetic wound can be as simple or complex as you need. The simplest way of healing the wound can be to see and feel the place where you cut the cord and heal it with "light" the same way you would do a basic energy healing. Sometimes there is a residual cord from the person that did the cutting. This energy must be transformed and re-absorbed into the energetic system. I find that using energetic alchemy works best. Please review the text and exercise on energetic alchemy before the next exercise.

Exercise #54: Alchemical Healing of Wound

1. After cutting/resolving a cord stay in a state of meditation as much as possible.
2. Put a hand over the wound or piece of cord and see it turning black and feel it burn off the previous influence.
3. When the energy feels done, see the energy turn white and imagine feeling the energy of purification.
4. When the energy feels pure, imagine it the energy turning gold and feel the blessing of the gods/ancestors/Divine blessing that energy.

5. When you feel the energy is as blessed as possible, imagine that energy turning red and becoming something part of you that will strengthen you.
6. Absorb the energy into the place where the wound was, into your hands, or into your root chakra.
7. Cycle your energy.

Aftercare

Cord cutting can be emotionally and physically taxing. I recommend having an action plan for after the cord cutting. This includes anything from:

1. Having adequate hydration afterwards.
2. Comfort foods or snacks.
3. Blankets and pillows to cuddle into.
4. Making sure you have someone you trust to talk to after to help process emotions.

Self-love is at the heart of healing ourselves, so giving yourself some care is a great way to help recuperate after an intense cord cutting. With spiritual work, you can go as deep as you are willing and able to dive. The more intense the process, the more aftercare you should have. What may take minutes for one person, may take hours or days for another. Everyone has their own pace, and you should honor your own process no matter what shape that becomes.

Other Uses of Cord Cutting

Cord cutting can be done quickly with practice. For example, if someone gave you the "evil eye" or you had a bad interaction with a stranger, you could cut the cord quickly to rid yourself of their influence. Cord Cutting is also useful in daily energetic maintenance to take care of any unwanted connections made at random. Think of it as psychic hygiene.

Chapter 9

Advanced Protection Magick

Summary: Advanced Shields, Advanced Warding, Creating Thought Forms, Advanced Banishing, Using Portals, Curse Removal and Reversal, Psychic Martial Arts

Advanced Shields

We went over basic types of shields earlier, and since you should have some practice moving and shaping energy, we can go over some advanced techniques. Personal shields can be changed at any time, and it is fun to experiment with different types. Will and imagination are the only things holding you back typically. Below are shield ideas and exercises for some advanced ones.

Exercise #55: Active Filtering Shield

I like this one especially when talking to someone that is filled with negativity whether it is someone like a co-worker or a family member. The theory is that make your shield like the standard screening one, but actively focus on taking in any useful energy and leaving the negative on the other side of the screen. The difference in active versus passive filtering is that you are drawing in the energy purposefully. In every interaction there is negative or un-useful energy, and positive or useful energy you can draw in. With shields like this and the Alchemical Shield below, you might notice how the other person you are dealing with "deflates" over time as they run out energy.

1. Center and be aware of your aura.
2. Feel the edge of your aura, and, where yours ends and the other person's begins.

3. Feel and visualize your aura like a filter or screen.

4. With every word from the other person, pull the positive energy consciously through the screen and leave the negative, or un-useful, energies on the other side of the screen.

5. If necessary, program the shield with your thoughts to ground out the negative.

6. With every breath, take in the useful energies and let the other energies stay behind the screen or be grounded out.

7. Keep this up as long as the interaction lasts.

Exercise #56: Layered Shield

This shield is good for extra protection. It is very useful to deter unethical psychic vampires or psychic attack since it can confuse people trying to attack you. There is the bonus that if something happens to a layer, there are back-ups. This exercise is for a three-layered shield, but you can do different takes on this. For example, creating layers using elemental energies (4 or 5), or layers that have different energies/sigils embedded in them. A variation is the "shedding shield" where you make many disposable layers that fall off after they have been attacked or interacted with something more than they can handle. Each layer can also be embedded with sigils for extra effect.

1. Cycle your energies between Heaven and Earth.

2. Center and be aware of your aura.

3. Hold your hand about 6 inches or 15 centimeters away from you. Feel and imagine a shield around you. Correspond this, and every other layer, with a certain color, key word, and/or sigil.

4. Hold your hand about the length of your bent arm away from you. Create a shield layer for that distance.

5. Hold your hand about the length of your outstretched arm away from you. Create another shield.

6. As you breathe in and out, imagine your shields becoming stronger and more solid. If necessary, cycle between Heaven and Earth to replenish yourself and put that energy into the shields.

Exercise #57: Alchemical Shield

This is a take on active filtering and layered shielding combined, but using the teachings of alchemical energy transformation. In this shield, literally anything coming from the outside world will make you stronger. This can also be used as a personal energy source in lieu of, or in addition to, cycling energies between Heaven and Earth. You can make this process as passive or as active as you would like or need to. What is important is the setup of the shields and using the breath to turn it on for the first time you use it. Once it is on, it is mostly self-sustaining. The only downside from it is that it can make the user very warm, and you may need to ground out excess energy.

1. Cycle your energies between Heaven and Earth.
2. Center and be aware of your aura.
3. Be aware of your space between you and the most outer edge of your aura. Measure out the space between your skin and the outer aura in quarters.
4. Place your hand to as far out as you can reach or to the edge of your aura. Visualize and feel a layer of shielding made of black fire to symbolize the Nigredo stage of alchemy – the stage of burning things down to their essentials. Any energy that touches that layer will be reduced to energetic "ashes".
5. Be aware of the space that is about a quarter from the last layer. See and feel a layer of white, purifying light to symbolize the Albedo stage of alchemy – the watery stage of purification. Energy from the last layer will be drawn to this purifying layer and become energetically clean.

6. Be aware of a space halfway between you and the outer shield. Construct a shield made of golden light. This is the bright and spiritualizing light of the stage of Citrinitas – the "yellow" stage of the purifying energy being blessed by the Divine. All the purified energy should come here to be reinvigorated spiritually.

7. Be aware of a space that is between the Citrinitas layer and yourself. This is where to construct a layer for Rubedo – the alchemical stage of "reddening" where the spiritualized energy is absorbed directly into your energetic system to strengthen you.

8. Breathe in and out. As you breathe in and out, see and feel this alchemical transformation of energy coming to you from the Nigredo, through the Albedo and Citrinitas layers, and to the Rubedo layer. When the energy gets to the last alchemical layer let it strengthen and empower you.

Exercise #58: Healing Shield

This is a useful shield when you are in the middle of doing a series of healing workings, or just need to replenish yourself or your aura. This can be programmed to heal your aura, a chakra, or even your physical body. Remember with physical healing, energy work is a supplement to physical medicine.

1. Cycle your energies between Heaven and Earth.
2. Center and be aware of your aura.
3. Visualize your aura turning a color of healing (I like green) and imagine what your mind, body, and energy would feel like if you were as healthy as you could be.
4. When you next cycle your energies between Earth and Sky, imagine that the top of your aura is opened to the Sky, and the bottom is open to the Earth. With both ends terminating as points to "seal" the aura.

5. As you breathe in visualize and feel health coming to you from Above; as you breathe out visualize and feel any disease, sickness, or un-wanted energies being grounded to the Earth.

6. Leave in place, and discard or re-absorb when finished.

For any of these shields, proper maintenance will probably be needed. The easiest way is to gather enough free energy from circulating between Earth and Sky, or any free energy surrounding you that you can purify. Your shield is a magickal tool, and as such should be handled with some care. From here on out, I will skip cycling and centering unless they need extra focus.

Exercise #59: Offensive Shield

Sometimes you need to work offensively, instead of defensively. I find changing the shape of your shield alone can deter someone. I have walked alone in cities at night and have had people cross the street to get away from me after I put spikes in my shield. While the shape can be important, the type of energy you put out matters most. This exercise asks you to draw on your own experiences to change your shield. A variation is having the energy be evoked outside of you, drawing that energy to you, and have it merge outside of you to your aura. This keeps you energetically cleaner. If you want to, you can read the sections on evocation from later, and come back to this exercise.

1. From your core, or from some energy you evoke from outside yourself, feel an energy that is either fearful, painful, or repulsive.

2. As you breathe in gather the energy from your center. As you breathe out, feel that energy come from your center to your aura and strengthening it.

3. Make a key word, or use a word of power, and a key color for this aura. Chant your key word or word of power until the aura becomes as solid as possible.

4. Discard, or banish, as needed.

Exercise #60: Positive Feedback Shield

This shield creates a positive feedback loop so that you are taking in negative energies, filtering them, and returning them back to the person. I have used this for the effect of cheering someone up, and helping people feel at ease in stressful situations. As with all techniques, it can be used negatively by accident or intent, so please watch what energy you are returning to the person on the opposite side of this shield.

1. Create an active filter shield.

2. Create a purifying layer (Albedo) between you and the filter shield.

3. As you breathe in, imagine you are using your breath to help take the energy in past the filter to the purifying aura layer.

4. For those few moments when the breath is held, you can keep the energy "neutral" or use your will and imagination to change it to a specific emotion.

5. As you breathe out, imagine, and feel the purified, or purified and transmuted, energy going from you to the person through the screen.

6. Discard shields when no longer needed.

Exercise #61: Projective Empathy Shield

Empathy is two-sided coin. It can be receptive and projective. This shield can mimic natural charisma when used properly, and make people feel better in your presence. It can be used offensively and defensively.

1. Make a two layered shield – one inner and one outer.
2. Charge both layers with a single emotion.
3. As you interact with people, extend the outer shield towards them to envelop them.
4. As you breathe in, take in any excess energy from the place or people around you, to the place between both layers – feel and imagine it transmuting to the energy type of your chosen emotion.
5. As you breathe out, send the energy out to the people inside your outer shield.
6. When done, retract the outer shield to the inner one.

Exercise #62: Spinning Shield

Sometimes you do not want to interact with the energy you are trying to shield from at all, and even having a shield is not enough. In these cases, there is the spinning shield that repels all energy it interacts with. This can be active or passive.

1. Make a standard shield.
2. See and feel any energy coming around your aura (not interacting with it) and spinning counterclockwise.
3. Use your breathing to activate the shield, so that breathing out brings the energy towards your aura and breathing out takes it from you.

Exercise #63: Psychic Armor

Psychic armor is some of the thickest of armors you can create and use. It can be simple like a suit of armor or be as complex as something from an armored superhero.

Simple
1. Make an inner and outer layer of shielding.
2. See and feel the outer layer as a suit of armor, use your hands to sculpt it as necessary. Take as much time as necessary.

3. Make a third layer outside the armor and shrink it to cover the armored layer. This holds the armor together and seals it for added durability.

   Optional – program the armor to appear with key words or when you are in certain situations.

Advanced
   1. Make an alchemical shield.
   2. Sculpt the Rubedo, "strengthening" layer to be armor. Program with intent for the alchemical shields to power the armor.
   3. Surround the armor in a wide external shield that can be changed to any offensive mode or intent.

Advanced Warding

Much of what we have practiced with shields can apply to wards as well. Earlier we used sigils to ward and protect an area, the follow exercise is just one example of what you can do with the basic tools of energy manipulation we have gone over.

Exercise #64: Warding the Corners

This exercise applies no matter how many corners a room has. It is important to do both the top and bottom corners.

1. Gather some energy in your hands. Program it with the energy and intent of keeping you safe and repelling any intruder.
2. Send energy to each corner.
3. Draw an X to connect each corner so that each wall, the floor, and ceiling, are covered with a giant X on each side.

Variations include programming the energy in your hands with a specific planetary energy (for example, Mars). I knew someone that would watch horror movies before warding to get the energy of fear in their wards.

With wards, you can also just throw a giant shield around your home, or even go outside and cast a protective circle outside of it. In this case, your home can have inner and outer layers of shielding. I have cast a "haunted house" shield where my home emits a spooky vibe to scare unwanted guests away. Wards, and shields for that matter, can be selective if programmed to do so. If you were doing a double layer of shielding for your home – one repels unwanted people and energies but let in the ones that you wish.

Creating Thought Forms

One of the best ways of warding your home is to create your own thought form guardians. Thought forms are beings made of energy that you create and give a sort of life to. They are basically artificial spirits under your control.

The major considerations in any thought form are:

1. Intent.
2. Timeframe.
3. Energy Source.
4. Place.
5. Destruction or Upkeep.

Thought forms require a specific operating system, like a computer. Our intent is what makes the operating system. If we do a thought form for protection, we must decide on where it will be. Will you put it above your door, or even have it stand outside your home. We might give it the specific intent of warding off people that would do harm to those that live in the home. It is a common observation among magickal practitioners that the more specific the intent, the better results one gets. This is very true with thought forms, and is not just a guideline, but a requirement. While most spellwork can be compared to modern technology, thought forms are like magickal robots that must be programmed to do specific tasks. The story of "Jeeves" illustrates this.

"Jeeves" was a thought form that my roommate and I made to protect ourselves from people that did us harm when we lived in a rough neighborhood. He was given the task of scaring off unannounced visitors. He did his job exceptionally well; except we were not specific enough with our intent. A good friend of ours came to visit without telling us, and she took one step on the porch of our house and could not even make it to the door. Jeeves did his job well, but he was not programmed with any allowance to let in unannounced friends! The lesson is that the more specific the instructions are, the better the results.

The reason you make the thought form starts off with its purpose. In this case protection is what we are focusing on, but you can create a thought form for healing, prosperity, luck, love, or anything else. They are really living spells.

The energy that a thought form "feeds" off can be from anything. A friend of mine would make thought forms from things such as the joy of a child or the energy of rain. This influences the thought forms mannerisms, energies, and sometimes the way it performs its function. I have used my own personal energy to feed thought forms at regular intervals, but due to its vampiric quality, and the danger of a hungry thought form, this might not always be best.

Thought forms must be made to a specific time frame. If I was creating a thought form to bring me love, I might set the time frame to something for a week or month so I can see practical results. For a long-term project, you would need to find a way to "feed" the thought form energy for it to maintain itself, and just as if you were using a long-term shield, a thought form will need maintenance. Most magick is powered by the energy of the practitioner, and with thought forms they need energy to do their work and maintain their integrity. You can give a thought form an alchemical shield to maintain itself, have it absorb general or specific energy types from its immediate environment, or feed it energy on your own.

On a practical note, one must decide where the thought form will live. You could have them live at a certain physical location – such as outside your home or above your door, inside a layer of your personal shielding, or in an object. For the sake of informational purposes, a thought form tied to a physical object can technically be thought to be a golem. These can be as simple as a clay doll, or as complex as a sculpture. Really any object with an animated magickal spirit could be a golem.

When your thought form has served its purpose, it must be destroyed. This can be as simple as absorbing the energy, or "banishing with extreme prejudice". This must happen, otherwise random semi-aware magickal energy will just be floating around and causing trouble. This brings me to the death of "Jeeves" and why upkeep and destruction are important. My roommate and I, like some young adults with too much going on, neglected to feed "Jeeves" for some time. He needed to "eat", so he went into the habit of popping up at random times and scaring our third roommate and using their fear to feed from. At that point we knew we had to decommission "Jeeves", and we did so by thanking him for his work, breaking down his energetic form, and grounding the pieces to the Earth. Now it is time to make your own "Jeeves", but without the problems I had when starting out.

Exercise #65: *Making a Thought Form Guardian*

1. Decide on an intent. I like using a statement of intent that begins with "It is my will that. . ." and fleshing out my purpose afterwards.
2. Decide on a timeframe and energy source.
3. Gather energy and put into the shape of a person. Decide on size.

4. Give your thought form a name and tell it its purpose.

5. Tell your new thought form to do your will as decided by your magickal intent.

6. End with a statement of affirmation (such as "so mote it be").

You can also use the sigil and word of power method to make a thought form by the following process:

1. Create a statement of intent, subtracting the repeating letters. For example, "It is my will, that I am protected from any harm."

2. Decide in timeframe, energy sources, and upkeep.

3. Arrange the unique letters into a word of power and a sigil. Use the word of power as the name of your thought form (so try to make it as simple as possible, or even use an acronym).

4. Use the sigil in the air and charge it by chanting the name of your thought form.

5. When you have raised energy speak your statement of intent and speak directly to the thought form. For example, "It is my will, that I am protected from any harm, and you [name of spirit] will make that happen."

I have made thought forms for energetic alchemical purposes where the thought form takes in negative emotions and transmutes them into joy; semi-permanent guardians that guard my home; and ones to seek information and bring it back to me. Your will and imagination are the only limit.

Advanced Banishing

Earlier when we talked about banishing with things such as tones, sigils, and words of power there is a specific magickal theory we are employing. Everything is energy and energy is shaped by intention. That intention can also be information in its most basic sense. We use magickal techniques to disrupt the energetic intent or information. When we banish with a tone, the information is what is banished, not the energy. When we use energetic alchemy, the destructive fires of Nigredo burn away the information that the energy it contained and was shaping it. Advanced banishing can be said to be about disrupting the information with more force.

I lived in New Mexico for a time with my mother and stepfather. It just so happened that down the street lived one of my mother's friends that had a spiritual problem. She was living in a house she thought was haunted. Soon after they moved in, they heard noises, but what was odd was that the longer they lived there, the more tired all the residents of the home became. After hearing her story, I decided to investigate. The house was indeed haunted. Very haunted, but not just by the spirits of the departed, but by dark entities made of shadow that may have been causing the physical issues of the people that lived there. After my initial investigation, I made plans to help with the entities there. For the spirits of the departed, I created a portal (more about portals next) for the dead to pass through. For the negative entities, I focused a beam of aggressive, red, Mars-like energy towards them to break them up and destroy them. I know it sounds a little crazy, and I would have thought I was, except that my mother's friend and all the people that lived there got better. Their energy returned and their moods improved.

Exercise #66: Banishing Negative Entities
1. Construct a thought form for the purpose of "target" practice.
2. Create an energy ball and summon aggressive, forceful energy between your hands. Let it grow, accumulate, and charge. This energy can be customized by color, feel, etc.

3. Use your will and imagination to change the energy ball into a beam of energy directed at your target.
4. See, feel, and imagine your target being destroyed.
5. Purify self and the immediate space when done.

The above can be customized by sending the destructive energy as particles, sending it with the drawing of a sigil and sending the sigil with force, or even wrapping your hands in the banishing energy and "punching" the spirit in the air.

Another technique that I have employed is to make a hole in the spirit. This is usually accomplished by creating an energetic tool, such as a sword with a triangular blade, and using that tool to "deflate" the spirit. I say a triangular blade since it makes a nice three-dimensional hole in the offending spirit that cannot be healed very easily.

Sometimes we do not want to banish and destroy a spirit, but instead contain it. In that case, I would recommend using an object to contain the spirit. Some spirits can be "re-programmed" to your purpose, for others you may just end up destroying the object to destroy the spirit. Personally, I have used crystals to contain spirits in such a manner. My method is to imagine either a portal inside the object and the vacuum power of the portal "sucks" the spirit in or key the hand I am holding the object in to have an active, "sucking", receiving force and using the object to hold the energy I have summoned in my hand. This brings us to the subject of portals.

Using Portals

Portals are magickal openings between the physical realm and the spiritual. These are constructed of energy and driven by your mind. The portal I use the most, is to the realm of the departed – a place I am familiar with from doing ancestor work and trance journeys there. I find it a peaceful and effective ways to help spirits cross over.

There are a few tips and guidelines to make portals more potent and useful:

1. Portals are most effective when you have been to that place. We talk about journeying to other spiritual realms in the next chapter, but an effective place to make a portal to is the center of the Earth, with which there should be some familiarity from learning the art of grounding.

2. Portals are most effective when crated with the energy of the physical area you are in combined with the energy of the place the portal is to. Portals are liminal spaces, an in-between area at the threshold of both places. You are creating that portal with the neutral energy of where you are in the physical world and the type of energy from the place you are going to.

3. Portals should be temporary and open as little a time as possible. A permanent portal would be messy at best, destructive at worst. Just as you would not leave a magickal circle up, you should deconstruct your portal as quickly as possible.

Exercise #67: Banishing by Portal

1. Make a thought form for the purpose of practicing banishing.

2. Ground and meditate on your connection to center of the Earth – seeing and feeling with all your being.

3. With one hand, draw a circular portal in the air between you and the target. The portal can be of any distance from you and be off to the side or above the target instead of directly in front of you. Visualize the opening away from you and towards the target.

4. Imagine and feel the portal sucking the target into it. If you are having problems with this, visualize and feel the energy of the portal moving clockwise. Make the portal spin as much as possible. If needed, use the act of breathing in to remind you what energy being drawn to you feels like, and use that to program the active sucking of the portal.

5. See and feel your target going into the portal.

6. Uncast the circle in the similar manner in which it was created.

7. Purify yourself and the space.

Some points of caution should be handled with portals. The portal is shaped by your intent, so always focus your attention on the intent as much as possible. It is more likely for your portal to not work than for your portal to go out of control, like something from a fantasy novel or movie. Please use your judgment when using a portal, and do not use them on people. The only time I would use them with a person is to banish spirits in a person. In that case, I would have the portal above them and use energy to help assist the spirit into the portal. This is an extreme situation, and I would recommend getting professional, spiritual help in case something like this does happen.

Curse Removal and Reversal

Curses and deliberate, or accidental, magickal attacks can happen. While most energetic attacks are simple, some are as complex as the practitioner that did the work. As such, below are some is what I have learned:

Energy is energy. When someone does a candle magick spell, asks spirit to harm you, or any other magickal attack, the result is an energetic change. As such, we can remove or heal any damage done to our energetic bodies.

Curses can happen by accident. Magick can be done by non-practitioners all the time. A friend of mine was in an argument with someone online and the result were "spines" shot into their throat chakra. This was caused by a non-practitioner who just had enough emotion and focus to energetically attack. While the person meant harm, the non-practitioner did not set out to do a magickal attack, but it came from a reflexive reaction. Non-practitioners and untrained ones can do as much harm as someone who devotes plenty of study and time to magick.

You are not a victim. Magickal curse can be removed simply by finding the attack, dealing with it, and healing from the damage. You are not someone's personal "voodoo doll".

All that being said, here is a list of basic curses as they come up energetically, and how to deal with them. I am referencing how they often appear in the energetic body. Always do a thorough scan before and after working with curse energy. You should be able to use your second sight, in coordination, if possible, with scanning the energetic body with your receptive hand.

Energetic "darts" or "missiles" – These are typical of short spell bursts, or reflexive emotions. These often appear as solid, dark masses that are thin in nature. They can range from as small as a dart, to as large as an arrow. Some barely penetrate your shield, and as such you can simply discard and create new shields. If they pierce the energetic shield, cut open energetically to where it is and gently perform psychic surgery as outlined above. While some are mere annoyances, some can impede your energetic functions dramatically.

Tentacles – These breach the outer parts of your energy. They can cause damage to the physical body or take advantage of current physical medical problems. There are two main strategies – keeping the tentacle intact or cutting it from the source. If you are cutting it, take a firm grasp with one hand as you cut it off at the entry way, slowly pull it out, and then dispose of it. Purify the area and heal any wounds energetically with white light or with the like energy of the surrounding area. If you are not cutting the tentacle, then you must slowly remove it and plant it in a ball of energy – preferable like your energy so that the tentacle still has a target, but the target it not directly you.

Stabs and cuts – These can also be reflexive and are usually a sign of an attack from extreme emotion. If there is not a weapon to pull out, purify the area, heal, and seal with an energetic band-aid or in some cases visualize the area being stitched up. These can cause energy leakage when not treated, resulting in fatigue and moodiness.

Confusion, madness, or persuasion magick – These are typically aimed at the head. You may feel a tightness or "dryness" in the head, light-headedness, or become very spacey. The goal of these curses is drive you toward a behavior or emotion. These often appear as bands around the head, cords to the Third eye, or another energetic construct around the head. These can be dealt with by cutting away the energy constructs and disposing of them. Typical recovery is based on healing the afflicted areas (the aura may be "crushed" in some cases) and working on any Third eye or crown chakra damage. The best prevention of this is by being as stable as possible: eating right, getting enough sleep, personal and energetic hygiene. It is also good to do some personal self-evaluation and question yourself if your thoughts and emotions are your own.

Various energy constructs – Some curse will appear in imaginative shapes inside or outside your aura. Take care in feeling the energy before you destroy it, since some curse can radiate harmful negativity even when removed.

To reverse a curse, is to send it back to the original source. This source could be person, plane, or thing. Personally, most energy thrown at me I transmute alchemically and use it to strengthen myself. It seems the most karmically neutral solution. If you do want to reverse a curse, here is a procedure to do it.

Exercise #68: Curse Reversal

1. Identify the curse energetically in the body through scanning the energetic system.
2. Gently pull the curse out of you. Usually by the outer edge of its aura.
3. Take the curse energy into your hands and shape it through your hands or imagination into a dart, arrow, or some other projectile.
4. Will the dart to return to the person that sent the energy. You can say something like "return to sender" as you do it. You can use any gesture or method to deliver it.
5. Purify your hands, your body, and your space.
6. Do any healing work necessary on the wound and seal your aura. Create or maintain any necessary shields.

It is typically that simple. I would advise if something felt particularly nasty, you might want to get help from at least a fellow practitioner to have another opinion on your energies, go to an energetic healer or Reiki master, or just ask people to ask how you "feel". That is the thing about energy, everyone feels it and is aware of it some level and how you treat and defend your energy translates into all aspects of your life.

Psychic Martial Arts

Energy work can be used in more direct confrontations and defense. I call these psychic martial arts since energy is being used as if you were sparring physically with an opponent. I always advocate for finding a peaceful solution first through direct communication, kindness, and understanding. Sometimes "doing no harm" only goes so far.

For example, there was a person that was an unethical psychic vampire that kept trying to drain my friends and me. To combat this, I would synch my energy with theirs, very much using projective and receptive empathy to create an energetic circuit and ground as hard as possible. As a result I would be grounded and the vampire learned very quickly that they would be neutralized.

Here are a few techniques to contain a situation and resolve it quickly (along with defense against them):

Projective Empathy – Just as you can shield energy, you have the ability to project it. It is quite simple to project fear, or any other baneful emotion, to a target to ward them off. This is useful when you want to influence a target subtlety and when direct confrontation is not advantageous. Variations include transforming their aura directly, making a "cloud" of energy, or creating a cord from you to your target and sending energy along the cord. If using the cord method, do not forget to cut the cord when complete. Defense includes shields and personal reflection.

Psychic Vampirism – To be more direct, you can also drain the energy out of a target by creating an energetic cord and cycling energy. From there you would cycle more energy to you than you give back. Defense against this would be cord cutting and shielding, cycling your energy back to you, grounding the target out, and being aware of the energetic vampirism and consciously sending baneful energy through the connection until they stop.

Energetic Javelins – I have used this technique only in extreme situations. Here you would create an energetic javelin that you would visualize going through someone's chakra. For example, if someone was spreading a malicious rumor, you could pierce their throat chakra. Defenses include removal and extra shielding in that area, alchemical transformation of the energy, and any way you would deal with a magickal "dart".

With any magickal offensive act, please take caution. These should be last resorts. Follow your personal code of ethics at all times, and remember to not to leave yourself open to attack. In order to create energetic changes, we open ourselves to be sensitive to them in order to manipulate them. Remember to use your psychic defenses when needed.

Finally, please be careful of magickal paranoia. There is the danger that if you are always on the defense, you will see enemies where there are none. While there are sometimes people out to get you, this is the exception and not the rule in regards to how you would deal with most people. Most people are too busy messing up their own lives to mess with yours.

CHAPTER 10

Trance Journeying

Summary: What is Journeying? The Map, The Four Worlds, Metaphysical Real Estate and Cosmology, A Means to Travel, A Purpose, Safety, Guides, Trance Journeying, Astral Realm Journeying, Shape Shifting

What Is Journeying?

Journeying is the art of trance and spiritual travel. Spiritual journeying is one the more gratifying things one can do as a magickal practitioner. My first journeys were "shamanic" in nature at the direction of other "shamans". I put this word in quotes since the word shaman really refers to indigenous practitioners of Siberia and it has been appropriated by man outside of its original context. Most indigenous cultures have their own practitioners that go into trance states, go to spiritual worlds, and accomplish tasks to benefit themselves or others.

My first solo journey was to go to the Underworld and find a guide. I had a small frame drum and I visualized an opening in the ground. I beat the drum faster and faster until I found a steady beat that helped me get into a trance.

I felt like I was falling – falling into and beyond myself. At the entrance to the Underworld, I gave an offering and I asked for a guide. The first entity I met would not give me its name (or perhaps I was too spiritually immature to understand it) and I waited for a second one. The second guide was a fox, and it led me to the Underworld proper.

In the last chapter, I mentioned that portals are most effective when you have been to that place (and there are many). Journeying happens when we can move our consciousness beyond the physical and venture into other metaphysical places. It is possible to go to lands of the Fae, the spiritual realms of the Norse, even the places of our ancestors. However, we cannot just get into a meditation and travel. We need the map, a means to travel, and a purpose.

The Map

One of my favorite teachers said to me "do not confuse the map with the terrain". I had no idea what that meant until years later. What he meant was that there is the Universe, and there is you. Between us and the Universe there is a filter. This filter is made of our feelings, memories, and experiences. We both experience life through the filter, and how we live changes it in an eternal feedback loop like the ouroboros – or the snake that devours itself.

I want you to think of these filters and something can be interchangeable. All the systems of mental maps that exist – from astrology to tarot – are nothing but interchangeable filters that were created in an attempt to understand the Universe and our relation to it. With our mind, we travel these maps every time we study them. These maps typically reside not only in our thoughts but in what we call the Astral realm.

There is a spiritual and magickal law that comes to us from the ancient magician Hermes Trismegistus – "As above, so below". What this means is that not only what happens in the physical world is reflected in the spiritual, but it speaks of the relationship between humans and the Universe. As such the mental maps we create to explain Ourselves to ourselves, exist as much internally as externally. Each mental map represents a cosmology that you can interact with directly.

Since they are all maps of one Universe, each system has its own validity and worth. It is not to say that they are completely right or wrong – they are focusing on certain aspects of the Universe. It is impossible to mentally understand the entire universe, but we can learn different truths through our interaction with it.

There is a Hindu teaching story about a teacher that presents an elephant to three blind men and asks them one at a time what is front of them. The teacher puts the first blind man in front of one of the ears of the elephant and feels what is front him. He says, "This is the leaf of a palm tree". The second blind man is put in front of the tail of the elephant and says, "This is an interesting piece of rope." The third blind man is put directly in front of the elephant's trunk, and as the elephant touches the blind man's face and playfully tries to embrace his torso, he screams in horror and yells, "Stop! Get this giant snake of off me!"

The moral is obvious, but the point I am trying to make abundantly clear is to not confuse the mental maps we use as the entire terrain of the Universe. We are all blind people feeling the Universe with our limited senses, using imperfect maps to guide us that are created by mystics. Humility, care, and caution are the pillars of successful spiritual journeying.

The Four Worlds

Back in the beginning of this book, I spoke about the four bodies: the physical, the energetic/astral, the mental body, and the soul. If we use the key of "as above, so below" to unlock our awareness of the Universe – then we can see that the "below" of the four bodies corresponds to four different realms.

Terrestrial Realm/The Physical – Corresponding to the physical world. This is the part of the Universe that is about manifestation. It is in realm that the body that is born, changes and eventually dies. The physical is the ultimate expression of the spiritual.

Lunar/Energetic/Astral Realm – This is the realm of emotion and energy. This is the place where many spiritual objects, forces, and beings are easily accessible. There is a direct energetic correspondence between magickal energy we manifest and manipulate in the physical and energy of the astral. They are not only interchangeable, but they are also the same. Here your energetic body can be free, you can have experiences with other people, visit the departed, and interact with gods as it is their abode and intermediary space. This is also the realm of dreams.

Solar Mental Realm – The mental realm is the place of gods – both deified ancestors and archetypal elemental forces. The lunar and solar realms are thought to be reflections of each other in some schools. The difference between a solar body, and a lunar or astral one, is that the solar body can have your consciousness transferred to it directly at death and you will retain your individuality. In the mental realm, your thoughts are real.

Stellar/Soul Realm – It bears repeating that if there was an event that created the Universe, then at one point all is One. The seat of "all is One" consciousness is in this realm. There is no time. There is only one moment – the moment of Creation happening all at once.

Metaphysical Real Estate and Cosmology

The "four realms" are only one cosmology – just one map. All are valid. Below is a survey on a few of them in no particular order. Please do your own research. I could talk about my own experiences with these places, but I do not want to contaminate your personal experience with my own.

Four Elemental Realms – This the archetypical place of elemental energy – Air, Fire, Water, and Earth. The landscape matched the element, and the classical inhabitants are the sylphs (air), salamanders (fire), undines (water), and gnomes (earth). This is great place to start journeying since most witches, pagans, and occultists are familiar with the four elements.

The Chakras – The chakras in the body have an equivalent in chakra realms. You can visit deities of each chakra there, as well as experience the pure energy of that chakra on its own and be surrounded by it. I like to start in the root chakra and work my way up. Travel occurs along the sushumna.

The Nine Norse Realms – The nine worlds from Norse mythology are some of my favorite places to journey. The nine worlds of Midgard, Muspelheim, Niflheim, Jotunheim, Alfheim, Svartalfheim, Helheim, Vanaheim, and Asgard all offer unique destinations. I recommend traveling to them one at a time, starting at Midgard (the realm of humanity), going to the specific realm, and back again. I once assisted a friend to stay in trance for going through all nine worlds – and it took me at least nine hours! I would recommend reading several sources on the realms before attempting to journey.

The Planets – Each of the planets in astrology can be visited. Typically speaking, you will encounter the planetary energies in their purest form, like the chakra realms. I like to visit the seven classical planets since I have worked the most with them. The planets would be the Sun, Mercury, Venus, Mars, Jupiter, Saturn, Uranus, Neptune, and Pluto. While the planets are named after deities, I typically will interact with them mostly on the astral.

The World Tree – This is the cosmology of Underworld, Midworld, and Overworld. Journeys start at Midworld typically and most journeys are to either explore the spiritual nature and intersection of Earth and Spirit at they interact and overlap. Going to the Underworld is something that usually happens to visit the departed, find lost parts of the self, and gain information. The Overworld is the realm of the Sky – a transcendent realm of pure spirit where you can interact with "higher" spiritual beings such as angels, gods, and interact with planetary energies; this is very similar to the solar realm.

The Kabbalistic Tree of Life – Coming from Jewish mysticism and adopted into the Western Magickal system, the Tree of Life sections the Universe into ten "spheres of light" called sephiroth. These range from the physical world, to thought and emotion, to more esoteric facets of reality. The ten sephiroth are connected by 22 paths – paths that correspond to the Major Arcana of Tarot and letters of the ancient Hebrew alphabet.

A Means to Travel

Let us say you have decided on a map – let us say the four elemental realms of Air, Fire, Water, and Earth, and you want to meet the inhabitants there. You need a way to travel that map. There are several ways, and we must consider both the physical and energetic components.

The physical way to travel is based upon traveling between brain wave patterns. Trance journeying to different realms happens by way moving from one state of mind to another. The "best" spiritual experiences the deeper you can go while retaining consciousness. I think the best place to venture is somewhere between alpha and theta (see the list below) – right on that line. This does not mean that journeying in alpha is bad, and our conscious minds can mess with us if they are not clear and our emotions that are under the surface not dealt with.

Consciousness	Description
Gamma/Concentration	Where the mind is learning and problem solving
Beta/Wakeful State	"Normal" alert consciousness where the mind is active
Alpha/Meditation	Relaxed State of Consciousness where the mind is relaxed
Theta/Deep Trance	An in-between state where the mind is awake and is in deepest meditation

We must come to a state of meditation and deep relaxation, and then go further into trance. Some classic ways to get into trance is to lose yourself in the beating of a drum at a rhythmic pace (either one you play or music you play on an electronic device), trance dancing, and chanting. I personally like to do a mix of chanting and movement. I find that it stirs all my energy centers, and I can really let go. Once you decide on a technique on how to get into trance, you need to think about how you are travelling energetically.

When I am in trance, I will often visualize a way to the realm I am going to. It could be stairs that are carved into the ground, a boat that I am sailing on, or sometimes I just like to make myself a set of psychic armor and travel through astral "space". What matters is that there is something to key into your senses that a transition from one work to another is happening. While I find visualizations helpful, you can also feel the transition if you open your sense of energetic touch.

There are different schools of thought on what is most effective for trance, and I will present both so that you can experiment with which way works best for you. The first school of thought is that we should experience trance deep in the body, and the more in the body we are the deeper the trance is. The goal is to get into a "super mindful" trance where you are present not only in your body but grounded in your consciousness.

Exercise# 69: Deep Body Trance

Find a simple chant/phrase/word of power to repeat repeatedly. If you cannot decide one, try using the following chant/phrase:

As I chant, deeper and deeper.
Into my body, deeper and deeper.
Into my soul, deeper and deeper.

Optional: Get some background music, I recommend searching for any trance drumming that has a steady beat.

1. Start off chanting slow and get into a steady rhythm. Imagine the words shaping the energy inside of you allowing you to go deeper into your body and consciousness.
2. Stand if you are able, and start swaying back and forth. It does not matter if it is back and forth, or from side to side. Match the rhythm of your movements to the rhythm of your chanting.
3. Be aware of and move as many body groups as possible without disturbing your rhythm. Start with your feet and legs, and mover through the pelvis and hips, up to your arms and hands.
4. Be aware of your breathing – exhaling out more than you are breathing in.
5. Over time, let your awareness of your breathing, body, and mind melt into one.
6. Make your chant more intense – losing yourself to it and your movements.
7. When your chanting and energy reach a steady plateau, maintain it.

8. After you have been at the same energetic plateau for some time, chant slower until you are at rest to end your trance experience.

9. Rest, ground, and center as necessary.

If you use this ecstatic technique to journey, please take proper care of your body in terms of rest and hydration. If this was a full journey, you would visualize yourself taking a journey in whatever means you choose, arriving at your destination, then letting the energy plateau. When you are done with your journey, you would chant slower and slower until you successfully traveled back to neutral consciousness/beta state. You can have the energy climax during a journey, but typically this would happen at a dramatic part of the journey. For example, if you were in the Underworld retrieving a lost part of yourself, the energy may climax when you found and re-connected with that part. Although, I like to do things with as few tools as possible, it is possible to do this technique while using a drum or rattle.

To touch back on magickal theory, there are two major spiritual currents – one moving from Earth to Heaven and the other moving from Heaven to Earth. Another way to look at them is to view them as "manifestation" and "liberation". Energy that is contained in the Earth/Matter is liberated to the Heavens/Spirit; Spirit/Heaven manifests itself in the Earth/Matter/Physical. It is this back-and-forth transformation that is part of what powers magick. The previous deep body technique more helpful in grounding spirit, such as in invocation magick (next chapter) where for example, you may want to draw upon the energy of deity.

The other school of thought on trance is that of a more mental process, and similar to what people call astral projection. The idea is still the mind, project your awareness outside of the body, and have your consciousness journey as your astral and energetic body. Your awareness is focused in your astral body, and minimal awareness is in your physical body. This technique uses the liberating spiritual current to transport you to more subtle, spiritual realms.

Exercise #70: Astral/Consciousness Projection

1. Sit or lay down with your eyes closed.
2. Become aware of your breathing, and let it become as slow and labored as possible.
3. Imagine and feel a point of energy that is above you and in front of you.
4. See and feel that energy point as it expands.
5. Imagine looking through the point of view of that ball of energy and feel your consciousness getting more intense inside the energy ball.
6. Practice moving the ball with your consciousness inside of it. Move several "steps" to one side and then the other. Practice moving up and down.
7. If your mind wanders, focus on the energy ball and relax your breathing as slow as possible while being comfortable.
8. Let the energy ball and your consciousness expand as much as possible.
9. Try turning around as the ball of energy and look at your body.
10. When you are ready to return to your body, imagine the ball of energy sinking into your body. If you need a starting point for this process, try your crown and third eye – then go chakra by chakra to the root; you can also try your center and let the energy expand to fill your body.
11. Purify and ground as needed.

With this method of consciousness projection, you can move yourself anywhere – from spiritual realms to doing remote viewing in the physical world. It is useful since you can do this with minimal tools.

Sometimes a friend will ask for healing work, and they are long distance. Instead of sending healing energy to them, I may astral project to where they are and do healing work. If you are doing such a thing, I recommend starting out with simple energetic proof that you are working with the person. For example, I will project while I am on the phone with someone and try to tap their shoulder energetically. Then I will ask my friend if they feel me tapping on their body, or at the very least which shoulder. It is beneficial to do such things to sync up if you are doing any non-solitary work.

A Purpose

One should have a purpose to their journeying, even if that purpose is exploration. Decide on the best route to take on your metaphysical map in order to accomplish your purpose. Some purposes are exploration, knowledge, blessings, visitations with spiritual beings, and do healing work for your yourself or others. Using a statement of intent might be useful before beginning the work.

Safety

I would like to make an emphasis on safety. When journeying, please employ some basic safety methods such as purification and protection. Also, I feel that you get out what you put in. Since everything is connected, I try to put out good energy. Sometimes you need to practice self-defense and set firm boundaries. Please use good judgment in what you do.

When going to new places, I recommend a general attitude of respect and gratitude. If you feel overwhelmed, or need a break, you can journey back to where you started at any time. Please remember all the techniques for self-defense can be used when journeying. If you have a friend or coven mate that is willing, you can also have them watch over your body while your journey. This serves as a nice "safety net" in case you get overwhelmed. Depending on the intensity of your journey and your purpose, you may want to prepare for spiritual aftercare.

I try to prepare as much as I can in journeying. It is not uncommon for me to go on a journey to some place new in a full set of energetic armor and armed with energetic weapons as a safety measure. I find being prepared is the best course of action.

Guides

One way to help with your safety, and something I highly recommend in all journeying, is to have a guide. Spiritual guides can be ancestors or other departed loved ones, deities, "spirit animals", angels, or any other spiritual entity. Sometimes guides come to us when we are ready. When approaching unknown guides it is important to ask what they would like to be called and their intent. This helps catalogue guides for future experiences and helps align the guide with any clear purpose you have. For example, I may call upon Apollo to help with healing work since that is one of his attributes.

The next exercise is to help you find a spiritual guide. This is probably not your only spiritual guide as most people have several to call upon (most they might even be aware of). Either the trance or astral methods may be used.

Exercise #71: Finding a Guide

1. Use either the trance or astral method to get into a stare of journeying. Close your eyes if possible.
2. Visualize and feel that you are going to another place of your choosing – this could be place you know well or an imaginary place.
3. While in trance, as if there is anyone that can help you on your journey.
4. When approached by an entity, ask their name, and if they can assist you. If the entity does not feel helpful on

an intuitive level – simply ask it to leave. If they do not leave voluntarily, then banish.

5. When you find a helpful entity, try to get as much information as possible. What does it look like? Do they have a name? How do they communicate?

6. After communing with your guide, thank them, and respectfully journey back to your normal consciousness slowly.

7. Open your eyes and ground.

Your relationship with your guide is as simple or complex as you could imagine, and just as you begin and end relationships with humans, you can do so with guides. Do not feel obligated to work with just one guide, or even work with a guide more than once if it does not feel right. Your intuition is the best judge on what is right here.

You can also make a thought form to help you. Make sure your intent is clear and follow all the directions for thought forms. A thought form can be used as a navigation system, energetic storage, defense, or act as any tool that you might find helpful.

Trance Journeying

Trance journeying is often called ecstatic since we are cultivating a sense of body centered rapture. The backbone of this technique is the deep trance exercise above.

Exercise #72: Trance Journey to the Underworld

1. Get into a deep body trance.

2. Visualize a place, real or imaginary, where there is an opening into the ground. As you descend into trance, descend into the opening in the Earth. You can do this with or without visualizing a means to travel.

3. Let your energy increase in intensity as you travel. When you feel you are at a threshold between where you were,

and another place let your energy plateau and level out –
you can stop chanting when this happens but keep the
movements up to stay in trance. If you can stay in trance
while not moving, then this is optional.

4. Ask for your guide to accompany you, if possible.

5. Visualize the threshold between your traveling and
   the Underworld. This may be a gate, a door, or even a
   guardian. Respectfully ask to enter, you may want to
   visualize a gift to be left at the threshold or with the
   guardian. Pass with respect.

6. Enter the Underworld and explore. Listen to advice from
   your spiritual ally.

7. When you are ready to leave, go back the way you came,
   thank any guardians or spirit of the place.

8. Slowly journey back to normal consciousness – as you
   head back, you come back to a neutral meditative space,
   and finally open your eyes.

Astral Realm Journeying

The astral realm is a place of infinite possibilities and is both
around us and transcendent of us. It is made of the same energy
that we have been using this entire work, as such your will and
imagination can shape it. I use the astral as a launching point
for exploring different metaphysical maps. Since this realm is
all energy, you can do wondrous things such as create your own
astral places, send energy from the astral realm to the physical
world, or use it store energies for later. It some ways, like our
energetic bodies function as our "double", the astral realm is
like a layer of reality superimposed over the physical. It is easy
to access since it is the realm of emotions and imagination.

You can journey to and through any place on the metaphysical
maps. Please take caution as some places are only available
through others. For example, on the Kabbalistic Tree of Life,

it is best to journey in a certain order. Your journey through a map does not have to be on one setting – you can take up the journey where you left off if need be.

Exercise #73: Astral Journeying (Root Chakra)

1. Project your consciousness in an astral manner.
2. Imagine that you are travelling to a place outside of time and outside of space. You may want to chant "outside of time and outside of space" if you need assistance.
3. When you are in an "empty" space, begin to visualize and feel that you are at a familiar place, or one you imagined.
4. From your astral place, see and feel that you are travelling into the root chakra of the Universe.
5. Take note of your surroundings. What colors are there? What entities do you interact with?
6. When you are ready to end your journey, thank any entities and go back to your astral starting ground. Imaging you are grounding out any energies there and return to your body. Opening your eyes if closed.
7. When I journey to the root chakra, I often meet Ganesh – the Hindu deity most associated with the root chakra and new beginnings. I usually see everything as the red of the root chakra, and the more I am there, the more grounded and relaxed I feel. Journeying to each chakra makes chakra healing more effective since you are more in tune with the archetypal energies. You can also open portals to the Universal root chakra and draw those energies in any healing work directly from here.
8. Everyone's journeying experience can vary greatly. There is one metaphysical map that most people take for granted – our own reality filter. Most of us have biases, memories, and experience that change how we perceive people and situations.

9. It is also possible to journey as a group. I was in a coven with some friends, and we would meet up in an astral place specific to the group of us and sync each other's minds and consciousness through a round of energy ball catch. Anything you can do in the astral alone, you can do as a group. It may take practice and time, but it is not only possible but very practical.

Shapeshifting

Sometimes I shapeshift to journey places. I find it useful to change my astral body to the shape of a bird for journeying or even into something like a bear for defense and protection. The astral body is all energy and thus can be shaped into whatever I need for any given situation. You never know what situation you will find yourself in astral travelling. Perhaps you shapeshift into a raven to hang out with Odin's ravens. Maybe you need to find something on a soul retrieval, and you need to burrow into the earth like a mole. The tools you need are as various as the places you might journey to.

Exercise #74: Shapeshifting

1. Start a journey with your chosen method.
2. Journey to a neutral place such as an astral place of your creation.
3. Ground into your astral body (instead of your physical).
4. Feel your astral body become to change shape, starting at your arms and legs, then your torso, and finally your head.
5. Ask yourself: How do your thoughts change? How does it feel to be in that body? Move about in your transformed body. Take note of your emotions and if they have changed.
6. When you are ready to transform your astral body to its original shape, take note of your breathing, and bring it to a slower pace.

7. Visualize and feel your body changing shape to its original shape. Go in reverse order – from head and torso to arms and legs.
8. Ground in your astral body.
9. End your journey and ground in your physical body.

You can shapeshift when you are not on a journey and contort your energetic body to the shape of your design, and it will typically bounce back to a human shape quickly. I have done shape shifting in the physical mostly as defense. Just to make sure I am clear; I am not talking about changing my body physically.

Journeying allows us to get direct experience with Spirit. Sometimes, I wonder if I am actually doing something or if it is all in my imagination. When I have doubts, I typically ask for a sign of some sort. That sign usually comes from some sort of spiritual synchronicity. For example, if I did a journey through the nine Norse realms and I meet a man with an eye patch, as Odin has one eye, then I feel as if the Universe and the gods are trying to tell me something and that my experience was real.

Chapter 11

Evocation and Invocation

Summary: Purposes of Evocation and Invocation, Spiritual Beings, Evocation in Practice, Spirit Boards, Invocation and the Five Stages, Inspiration, Aspecting, Oracling, Channeling, Possession

Evocation and invocation magick can be some of the most challenging yet rewarding aspects of magickal practice. Evocation is the magickal art of summoning something outside of yourself – such as calling elemental energy to draw from. Invocation is when you call a spiritual force to enter you to some degree. Elemental invocations would have you draw that energy through you. To think of it another way, evocation would be summoning a demon, while invocation would be getting possessed by it. Alright, please do not go and get possessed by a demon – that was just an example, but it does remind me of a story.

A few friends and I were taking turns leading rituals. One of my friends, let's call him "Alex", decided to summon, and get possessed by a Goetic demon. Goetic demons are infamous in the occult world. They are spirits that the legendary King Solomon, of Biblical fame, used to build his temple. To go off on a tangent, the temple is a metaphor for the perfected self and the demons that Solomon mastered can be seen to be reflections of himself that had to be mastered. Alex started the process of invocation, and we all chanted the name of the demon while he prepared himself. The invocation did not work at first, so Alex decided to fake it. During his performance, Alex changed from the "demon" to himself with a look of panic. The demon has finally come to possess him, and he was not ready for it. It was not until banishing at the end of the ritual, did he come to his senses. After that, he decided to never fake magickal acts again. It was not demonic invocation that was inherently bad. It was Alex's disrespect of what he was working with, his arrogance, and his lack of magickal integrity.

I find invocation work very exciting and rewarding. I enjoy being in ritual when deities are invoked. When someone draws a deity into them, it is a truly magickal thing. Our deities do not need to just exist in the spiritual realm, a practitioner can draw them into themselves, and people can meet and experience their deity face to face. Our gods can be with us, and we can commune with them in the physical world. I find this to simply amazing. I remember when the high priestess of my first coven did an invocation to the Goddess. Her face almost seemed to change as she channeled different aspects, and the energy was noticeable different. My high priestess did not just act as a deity, she felt like it completely. When she blessed the food and wine we had for ritual, it tasted more intensely. It was like the food really tasted and felt touched by a deity.

For me personally, invoking a deity into me is very close and personal. I feel like I am touching a mystery and am part of it. There is no question of faith – I have literal proof that my deity is there.

As much as I enjoy ritual with invocation, I enjoy being possessed as well. There is a special relationship when you let something into your body like that. There is an intimacy, and a knowing of that deity that is beyond faith and goes into the experience of union.

Purposes of Evocation and Invocation
Typically, the practitioners will evoke spiritual forces to draw upon for the purposes of energy, information, and completing

magickal tasks. The classic evocation that popular culture likes to employ is someone summoning demon. While this is very possible, there are many more entities that evocation works with. For evocation, I like to summon spirits that will help me and others. If I was doing a prosperity spell, I might evoke gnomes to help as they are magickal creatures associated with Earth which is the main element connected with money, prosperity, and manifestation. Gnomes are also benign and easy to work with. A rule of thumb a teacher of mine used to offer was "do not summon something you are not willing to banish". To me, this means that I should not evoke that which I am not willing to deal with the consequences of.

I usually evoke an entity to aid in a magickal a purpose or for information. My old magickal partner and I used to evoke the archangel Michael to banish spirits that we were having problems with on our own.

Invocation has many different stages to it. When someone is doing spiritual mediumship and speaking to disembodied spirits, they are doing a type of invocation where the spirits are drawn into them to a degree that they practitioner still has most of the control. I have used invocation to a lesser degree to help with getting information I could not normally access. If I wanted to get a feel to see what energetically happened to a place, I might do the lightest type of invocation where I am inspired by the spirits of the place to understand what transpired. I would not recommend invocation for every situation. Much like the relationship between magick and trance, the deeper you go with invocation, the more effective it is.

Spiritual Beings

There as many types of spiritual entities as there are types of people. Below is a catalogue of the most common ones you may come across.

Deities – The gods are typically spiritual beings that have dominion over a specific field of human experience. For example, The Greek Aphrodite and the Norse Freya are deities that preside over love among other things. Theologically speaking we could make a difference between deities that seem to be more deified ancestors than incarnations of natural forces like the lunar goddess Selene, but the difference has no bearing how you can work with them. As they are the most human of spiritual beings that one can deal with, they are extremely approachable. Deities can have as many likes and dislikes as incarnated humans can have. When working with them it is useful to treat them as much as you can as people. Your relationship with deities can vary. I have found great progress having a relationship with deities as guides, mentors, substitute parents, and even lovers. As with any entity it is good to have clear, healthy boundaries and build on a foundation of respect.

Angels & Demons – While angels and demons seem to come from a more Judeo-Christian paradigm, any Pagan or occultist can work with them. I personally see them more as the personifications of the inner virtues and vices that are within all of us. I have found that angels are not all "love and light" so treat them with the respect you would give any spiritual being. For demons, I recommend banishing before evoking and after. I have noticed that without proper banishing, I tend to be obsessed with whatever that demon oversees. I do not feel that angels and demons are inherently good or evil. I tend to view all spiritual beings as neutral but shaped with our intent – whether that intent is positive and constructive or mostly negative and destructive to our progress as spiritual beings, seeking personal development and growth.

Elementals – Elementals are the spirits of an element, planet, or other occult environment. These could be as simple as the sylphs, undines, salamanders, and gnomes of the elemental planes or the spirit of heavenly bodies like Jupiter or Mars. These relationships tend to be straightforward, and I would caution on making sure you are banishing or do some purification afterwards so that you are not overtly under that elements influence at the expense of your own thoughts and feelings.

Nature Spirits – These are the spirits of stones, plants, rivers, mountains, and any other natural place. Most Pagans are animist in nature – meaning that we tend to believe that everything has its own energy and personality. I have found that communication with nature spirits tends to be raw and "clean". When I evoke a nature spirit, I like to communicate with it in their actual location. For example, if I was evoking the spirit of a tree, I would prefer to do it at the actual tree. You can evoke nature spirits to an indoor space, and when I have done that, I have felt that I am back at that place. For me, evocation of a nature spirit is less formal, and I am more bringing my consciousness to that of the nature spirit than I am calling it forth. Evoking a nature spirit is a good way to get into more direct communication with it, and use that ally's help even when you are indoors.

Animal Guides – Theologically speaking I feel that sometimes I am working with a spiritual guide that manifests as an animal as opposed to working with the soul of an animal. In this case it could have been someone that was once human, a deity, or some other spirit that is taking animal form. On the other hand, I have dealt with animal spirits where I feel that

I am working with the "main god" of that animal species. Once I was dealing with an infestation of ants, in a place I lived, but I did not want to resort to pesticides. I went into trance and communed with the "Ant Mother", and within a few days the ants had left the area. Animal guides have their own distinct personalities, and it is useful to treat them as people and not as pets.

Ancestors and the Departed – The mighty dead are always with us. Just because someone passes away it does not mean that your relationship with them, or the love you shared, goes away. I have an ancestor altar at home, and I routinely evoke those that have passed with prayer to watch over my family and me. Evocation does not have to be an elaborate ceremonial affair, it can be simple yet meaningful. I will rarely evoke the dead as I would another spirit, but it is something I might do if it is not one of "my" departed, and I need to communicate with them. For example, if you need inspiration you might want to invoke the genius of someone in that field to assist you.

Thought forms – We talked about constructing thought forms in a previous chapter, but like any spirit they can be evoked and invoked. I was the occult consultant on a movie that was about a medium that was possessed. For the film, I made a thought form of the "evil dead uncle" that possessed the medium. I then helped the actress that played the medium get possessed by the thought form so she could get a feel for what possession might feel like in as real a setting as possible. Other occultists have used thought forms to test out their invocation ability and then disposed of the spirit when the practice was complete.

Evocation in Practice

I do evocation in a few different ways. Before I go into technique, I want to go into theory, so you know exactly where I am coming from. Knowledge is power right?

Between the spiritual realms that exist outside of me, and the realms that house the spiritual beings I interact with and evoke, there needs to be a medium. That medium is typically energy. In earlier chapters we have gone over portals and journeying. In evocation we are asking the beings we might meet in journeys to come to the physical realm instead of us meeting them where they are at. The problem is that these spiritual entities need a body, if only a temporary one. If the entity has an astral body, it should be able to be asked to our space easily. If it does not, then the practitioner must provide ample energy for the entity to manifest at least in the astral. Astral energy and the energy of magick are the same, so having that entity manifest an energetic body in the physical is more than possible.

When I do evocation, I am also creating a liminal space of energy where it happens. Liminal spaces are those in-between spaces that are thresholds that occupy space in at least two different, and distinct places. Evocation can theoretically happen in any realm. I can travel to the astral, or some other realm, and summon an entity to that realm as well. This means I can be on the astral to do evocation work and it will be just as effective as doing it on the physical.

Purposes I have for evocation are asking requests (for example, asking my ancestors to watch over me that day), blessing items (such as having Dionysus, the Greek god of wine and intoxication – among many other things – bless wine for a party), or directly manipulating energy on your behalf (for example, having Bethor, the spirit of the planet Jupiter, help make your energy more confident if you are going to a job interview).

Be clear in your intention in working with that entity. Ask if there is a price other than energy that needs to be paid. For example, I worked with a spirit of Mars that asked for me to win in four fights, or conflicts, to charge a talisman of protection. These could have been anything from fist fights to beating someone at chess. There was a price to what I asked. If you are not willing to pay the price for something an entity asked, please do not feel the need to do it. You do not deserve to be bullied by anyone or anything. If anything, you are the one with the power since you summoned the entity and you control the portal.

The words you use to evoke, and invoke as well, are very important. They are a sort of magick spell all on their own. They should be polite, direct, clear, sincere, and full of emotion. An example would be "Hail Hecate, goddess of magick, I thank you for your presence. Please open the way to clear communication between myself and the departed, so that I may talk to my grandmother". Manners are a necessity. You would have good manners when inviting physical guest over, manners in the spiritual will be the difference between success and failure. The gods and entities we call upon are our allies, not our servants.

Here are the methods I typically will employ in evocation.

Prayer – Prayer is one the most common methods of evocation. When we pray, our intentions can reach across time and space to the realms of the ancestors, the gods, or anyone else. When I pray, I am shaping the immediate energy around me to be the place I meet those spiritual entities. This is why altars can be so important to keep up and keep clean both physically and energetically – they are a liminal space between our realm and others. When many pagans call quarters, they are evoking that element through prayer.

Astral Evocation – This is where I would journey to the astral, shape energy into a neutral space in that realm, and evoke the entity on the astral. I have found this particularly useful when the physical realm is unsuitable for evocation work or I am in a really deep state of meditation, or trance, when I am laying down.

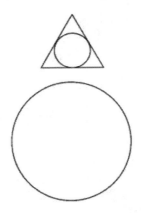

Physical Evocation – In physical evocation, I will make a traditional "triangle of manifestation" (pictured above) for the entity to appear within. The circle within the triangle is the portal I create. The subject is summoned with words, while energy is released to create an energetic body for the entity to inhabit (if it does not possess one). Even if the entity has an astral body, I will still offer energy to the entity to help it become as "solid" as possible. I typically only use the circle and triangle setup if I am evoking into the physical, but it could be used as part of any astral location that you set up for working there. I will usually make the portal so that it starts out inactive and it activates when I say appropriate words of power or prayers. I purify before the evocation, banish, have the interaction with the entity, then banish again. The purpose of banishment is to create as "clean"

an energetic area as possible for the entity to manifest in. During the actual interaction I will ask permission, do the work I need to do, and give a "license to depart" – which is basically saying "thanks for coming and I appreciate you". In physical evocation, it is traditional to have a scrying mirror and lots of incense where the idea is to have the entity come to physical appearance. I differ in tradition in that I will evoke into the triangle and communicate with the spirit back and forth in terms speaking aloud and receiving sounds and images psychically.

Sometimes I will communicate with a spirit with a spirit board or pendulum. I typically do not do this with deities, but instead will ask for feelings of a clear yes or no if needed. When I talk with deities, I will hear them, but sometimes it is only in what I call emotional aggregates of information – something like bits of information in the forms of images and feeling being sent to me directly.

Exercise #75: Evocation to the Physical

1. Before you begin, decide what entity you will evoke. Do as much research as possible.
2. Purify yourself and the space you are in. Banish energy from each quarter of your area with any combination of tone, words of power, and sigils.
3. Cast the triangle of manifestation and install a portal within it. If possible, cast a three-dimensional pyramid, but a triangle will work as well. Imagine that the portal is turned "off".
4. Use candles if needed at each of the three points of the triangle to aid in visualization of where it is at. You can also use candles around your circle.
5. Step back from the triangle, at least one step, and cast an energetic circle between you and the triangle.

6. Read, or recite from memory, words to invite the entity through the portal. These should be composed beforehand. Emphasis should be placed on emotion and sincerity. Imagine the portal "switching on". See and feel the entity being evoked from the portal. If the energy is feeling weak, "feed" the entity some energy to help manifest its astral body. CAUTION: Stop feeding as soon as you feel the entity has manifested to avoid energetic vampirism.

7. Thank the entity for its appearance. Verify their name and attributes.

8. Ask the entity what you would wish of it. Find out what price there is for the entity to help you. Accomplish any agreed upon magickal work if it is possible to complete within the circle.

9. After the body of magickal work you wish to accomplish is complete, thank the entity. Give them a "license to depart". Close the portal.

10. Reabsorb, banish, or ground out the energetic constructs that were cast. Banish the space and purify it and yourself.

11. Take any notes. If there was a "deal" where you must do something in the physical realm to keep your end of the bargain accomplish it as soon as possible.

You can change the boundaries of the outer circle to be as permeable or solid as you feel necessary – just like you would with any personal shield. In "feeding" entities, if you notice a drain on your personal energy, feel free to cut the energetic cords immediately. This is true if you notice odd obsessions. In any case, feel free to banish as necessary.

Deities and the departed are a little different for me in terms of relationship. I will have altars and leave offerings such as food and drink to "feed" them. This energy exchanges helps create and energetic bridge between them and me and strengthens the energetic cords.

My rule of thumb is the more unpredictable the entity, the more you want to have all the safeguards and protections. I feel that deities, being closer to the Source than we are, are above being evoked with a portal and I will pray directly to them or invite them directly into my space. My "license to depart" is always respectful and full of gratitude.

Spirit Boards

Spirit boards are a little different than normal tools of evocation. As I shy away from tool usage in this book specifically, I did want to talk about spirit boards since they are so popular and give some tips on how to use them energetically.

First off, a spirit board should have a portal installed within it. I also always visualize an energetic lock on the underside, and make an energetic key to turn it "on" when needed. I always keep mine in the "off" position for the sake of safety and good energetic hygiene. Once I left my spirit board "on", and my step-father touched it out of curiosity. He said he felt very cold, and he did not feel right in his body, and it took some banishing and healing to make him feel right again. Needless to say, I hope my carelessness serves as a warning.

Secondly, I typically will take all the precautions and setup of banishing before and after such as creating an energetic circle and asking for any spiritual help to be on hand as a backup. I find that I get less mischievous spirits, and I can talk to who I want to, when I have, for example, a deity of death or the boundary between life and death nearby. Never be afraid to ask for help from others – whether they are physical or spiritual.

Invocation and the Five Stages

Invocation is the magickal art of bringing a spiritual entity through you and into you to varying degrees. It is the opposite of evocation. Your body is the temple that the spirit inhabits. It is useful for getting answers directly, having them bless or enchant objects, or any other reason to commune with an entity directly.

Invocation can be a form of worship and connection. There are several preliminary steps to invocation. First is research. It is necessary to get as much information as possible on who or what you are working with. Secondary, is forming a connection before invocation or evocation work through meditation and perhaps prayer. Lastly, it is useful to build sacred space that sets the tone or mood of who you are working with. For example, you might want to call in the energies of Venus if you are working with a deity of love such as Aphrodite.

Invocation for me is as real as it gets for spiritual experience. I have worked with many deities and spirits, and I believe in prayer and meditation as ways to connect to the gods very easily. Invocation restores my faith and eliminates doubts. To actually have a deity, or some other spiritual entity, actually be present, fills me with wonder and awe. I have gone up to someone possessed and received information of the past and future that no human could have known. On the other side of that, when I have done invocation work, I am touched by that deity and understand it in a way that words could not easily express.

For one ritual, I did an invocation of Hephaestus – the Greek smith god. While I was possessed, I felt my limbs get heavy and they began to contort themselves in ways that they never had before. Hephaestus was thrown off of Olympus when he was young, so the myths say, and he was a deity with some physical disabilities because of that. When I was Hephaestus, I was supposed to bless ritual tokens by hitting them with a smith's hammer. I found that sometimes I made mistakes, or I would drop the token. It was then I had a spiritual realization, I felt all the way from my crown chakra to my toes: sometimes Hephaestus could work for a long time on something, even be almost finished, but his disabilities might cause him to make a mistake, causing him to start all over again. Later, I realized what I gift it was to see the world through the eyes of a god. I understood that everyone had the problem of Hephaestus – sometimes we could create something and our disabilities or flaws got in the way of that, and we may have to start all over whether it was a project or our very lives. By invoking the deity into me, in this case in the stage of aspecting, I learned some of his greater spiritual mysteries.

The vehicle for invocation to happen is trance. We talked about trance states earlier in meditation and journeying. The deeper you go into trance, the deeper the brain wave frequency you are headed for. For every type of invocation, you need to at least be at alpha state. The art of invocation is fairly simple: get into a trance, call the entity you want to come into you, go as deep a trance as you want the entity to take over, have that spiritual experience, and come back.

Depending on how deep you go, when you call a deity into you, you see how the world through their point of view. You can bestow the energy of that deity. It is possible to be their oracle. In my experience, I have found that there are six distinct levels of invocation (for the sake of simplicity, I will talk more about working with deity, but the following does apply to any spiritual entity you invoke): inspiration, oracling, channeling, and possession. They range from lesser to greater forms of invocation and increasing levels of letting the deity take over your own loss of control.

Inspiration

This is where you invoke the deity just above you, or barely into your crown, to all the way to your third eye. This is useful if you need literal inspiration for a project – like invoking the goddess Brigid when you need help writing a poem or need guidance on love from Aphrodite. It is possible to do divination while under the spiritual guidance that comes from this stage of invocation. I would caution that the inspiration you receive will be influenced by who or what you invoke. While I would probably ask Thor for inspiration on when to plant crops and what the best time for something related to weather would be, I would probably ask Hermes for business advice on a reading concerning investments. By the way divination involving a deity is theomancy.

Exercise #76: Inspiration for Divination

This exercise can also be used for inspiration on project of your choosing. Replace your divination method with whatever your medium is.

1. Choose your divination method (for example, tarot, runes, etc.) and the deity, or spirits, you would like help from.
2. Meditate and sit quietly. Slowly open your crown chakra.
3. Pray to the deity of your choosing. Thank them for their help. Give offerings if applicable.
4. Place your hands in your crown chakra briefly to charge them, and then start the shuffling, casting, etc., of your chosen divination method. This step is optional.
5. Open your crown chakra as much as possible, and imagine and feel the energy coursing through and opening your third eye.
6. Do the reading.
7. Afterwards, thank the deity or spirits. Close your crown chakra slowly.
8. Ground and center.

Aspecting

In this stage, you are drawing upon the energy of inspiration from above, to influence others directly as a representative of the deity. You are very much in control and you are carrying the energy of the deity, and not losing yourself to it. This stage of invocation is very effective when you need someone to represent a deity in ritual or magickal workings. The mechanics are similar for inspiration, except the energy of the deity would be more like a waterfall coming off the crown chakra and almost gently pouring off of the practitioner. It is also useful to imagine that the energy of aspecting is more like wearing a cloak that you clothe yourself in, than something you lose yourself to such as in later stages. Most use of aspecting is performative.

Oracling

Here the energy of the deity is coming down through the head to the throat chakra. At this point the crown, third eye, and throat chakra are all involved. To be an oracle of a deity is to be their mouthpiece. Being an oracle is all about letting the truths and wisdom of the deity come through. Since this is not a whole bodied possession, sometimes it is difficult to differentiate between what your truth is versus the truth of the deity. To counteract that, it is important to be as ego-less as possible.

If you feel your emotions, more than you are communicating in that invocation, you may need to take a step back from the process. It is better to take a pause to collect yourself and be a proper channel than to say something that is tainted or untrue. While this can be done alone, it is better to have someone present to help take notes of what you say – that way you can stay in trance and keep the results of your work.

Being an oracle is a large responsibility. It is best to do oracling and any other deeper invocation when you have a relationship with a deity, or at the very least trying to cultivate one. To speak for a deity, or any spirit for that matter, is significant work. When I started doing invocation work, it was at this stage I felt I began to take my practice even more seriously.

Oracling is very similar in practice to the previous invocation level except that the energy is brought down to and through the throat chakra. I recommend closing your eyes as to block out visual stimulation and to focus on hearing the spirit or deity. At this stage and on, you really need someone to assist. In oracling, you need someone to ask and record questions, and also help guide if necessary. When assisting invocation, I like to help people come back to reality when they are done, by asking them their name and a random question that uses their conscious mind like what year it is or where they live.

Channeling

You are about 50% still in control of your body at this point. In oracling, the chakra energy stayed at the throat chakra level; here it will rest at least at the 3rd chakra and from there flow into your energetic body. Channeling contrasts with being an oracle, in that the deity has more room to operate in. It is as if I am carrying the deity in my body more so that it is coming through me. Channeling is a great way to get in touch with deities when you need to not only communicate, but also handle physical objects. A deity may charge a talisman, give advice, or even do automatic writing. It is wise to have offerings at this level of invocation and deeper; after all the deity being there is a gift and as a way of showing good spiritual manners, it is good to have a gift. Gifts, especially of food and drink, nourish the practitioner's body and give energy to the deity directly.

Exercise #77: Channeling

1. Go through any preliminary grounding, centering, and sacred space set up.
2. Get into trance through meditation, trance dancing, or any other method that you find that works. Let yourself get deeper into trance the more you breathe in and out. Let your breathing be the key help you descend.
3. After you have reached a sufficient state of trance, imaging the energy of the deity above you.

4. As you pray or say your invocation, imagine the energy descending through your crown and all the way to your solar plexus chakra. Let the energy of the deity flow into your energetic body.

5. If you have a group, or assistant, they should thank the deity for their presence, and present any offerings.

6. Ask any questions, or petition for any requests.

7. Thank the deity for their visit and give them permission to depart.

8. If this was part of a larger ritual, proceed, otherwise banish, and purify the space and the practitioner.

Possession

At this point, the deity has come all the way through, is in your body all the way, and has about 90%-95% control. I say 90% to 95% since 100% is rare. The energy of the deity is fully descended into the body. I have found that there is still a spark of control within someone even at the deepest levels. It is best to communicate with the deity what your boundaries are and what you will not do no matter the situation. Having clear and direct boundaries with the is important in any relationship, and even more so where the deity is having control over you.

Possession should be done with a group. To get into the deepest trances, it is best to be surrounded by people in a light trance to help you invoke the deity. There is a type of spiritual resonance when people go into a group trance. It helps to have a group evoke deity into you, while you are doing the invocation. This group effort helps the practitioner get into deeper trance and awareness of the deity. Only do possession work with people you really trust, as you will be in a vulnerable state. Black outs and memory loss can happen, so be prepared for that.

I typically invoke in the direction of Heavens to the Earth, from the head through the body and to the feet, and sometimes working from the opposite direction of Earth to Heaven works best. I have found that invoking from the Earth is useful for when you are doing possession work – especially with land spirits, ancestors, and gods of the Earth/Underworld.

When I do invocation at this level, I find it useful to have a chant that you and the other participants can use easily. For example, if I was invoking Pan, the participants and I would chant "Io Pan" repeatedly. I would let the energy build so that at the climax of the energy being raised, the deity descends.

Exercise #78: Possession

1. Go through any preliminary grounding, centering, and sacred space set up.
2. Arrange yourself so that you are in the center of the circle, and everyone else surrounds you.
3. Begin the invocation chant.
4. Get into trance through meditation, trance dancing, or any other method that you find that works. Let yourself get deeper into trance. The other participants should get into at least an alpha state of relaxation, if not a little deeper.
5. Feel the energy of the deity above or below you. Let the energy from the chant get as intense as possible.
6. When the energy climaxes, let the energy of the deity rush into your body completely, filling you. As you are filled with energy, release any last bits of ego.
7. Someone from the group, or an assistant, should thank the deity for their presence, and present any offerings.
8. Ask any questions, petition for any requests or acts of magick.
   Thank the deity for their visit and give them permission to depart. Ask that the person be brought back.
9. After the license to depart, verify the person's name and ask any other bits of information to verify they are back in their body (for example, address, what year it is).

10. Banish and purify the space and the practitioner.
11. Give proper aftercare to the practitioner.

All forms of invocation should be done with care. As I have mentioned several times, it is best to do this in a group, and mandatory for possession. When you work in a group and have that experience face to face with a deity or other spirit – it can be a life changing thing. You can have Brigid with you at Imbolc or even have multiple deities channeled for a spiritual gathering (just make sure they get along first). Please be careful, but also enjoy the magick. Evocation and invocation work can some of the most satisfying magickal acts you accomplish.

Chapter 12

Spellwork and Ritual

Summary: Anatomy of a Spell, Spell Tips, Anatomy of Ritual

Spellwork and ritual are the summation of all the techniques that we have worked on so far. This is where are individual parts come together for a whole. While Spellwork can be part of a ritual, both follow patterns and are multi-layered. For me spellwork and ritual go hand in hand, as sometimes the main part of the ritual is the spellwork; spellwork can be enhanced by the different parts of the ritual.

This chapter is intentionally short. I want you to create your own rituals and spells based upon the techniques from the previous chapters.

Anatomy of a Spell

A spell is like a magickal child. It has a life all its own. It is born from our intent, nourished with magickal energy, carries out its life for the purpose of making our intentions real, and diminishes when it accomplishes its goal. Each part of the spell's life is important and should be carried out with great care. I find that most of the reasons my magick works is that I have all the parts of a spell all balanced out and have thought my process through beforehand. This is not to say that spontaneous magick is not effective, but even that is born out of experience in spellwork practice. The map I use to break down and plan a working is typically broken down into four parts:

Intent – Your intent drives everything in magick. Thoughts shape energy and keeping your thoughts in order and your intention clear lead towards more effective magick. I like to write a "statement of intent" and memorize it. For example, I will write something like "It is my will to make an extra $1,000 in the next three months." Using "it is my will", helps remind me to funnel all my determination and control into my magick. Besides, having a statement of intent can be used to make personal sigils and words of power.

Energetic Means – What is the energetic medium your spell is going to be? Are you working with cords, energetic constructs, chanting, sending energy directly, or something else? The energetic component is the body of the spell. Are you making a magickal dart? Are you sending a wave of energy? Are you making a thought form? I know I am asking a lot of questions, but your means should be as specific as your intent. In my example of making extra money – I could enchant my hand with luck energy before I picked a lottery ticket, I could send energy to my boss for a raise, or I could make a thought form that helped me make decisions that would create more wealth.

Release – The release is how we send the energy out into the world. This may be letting energy built to a climax and then released to the Universe, "planting" your intention in the Earth, sending it out to a specific person or direction, or releasing it in every direction. Different things work for different people, and I would advocate experimenting to see what works best. Magick seems to function in optimum ways objectively, and it is highly specific to the practitioner.

Physical Work & Result – I was taught that whatever magick you do, you must do the accompanying work or action in the physical world. If you are doing a spell to get a new job, it would probably be wise to put out resumes and apply for jobs. That being said, the Universe will often use synchronicity to make things happen. Synchronicity is the spiritual power of coincidence. For example, perhaps I do a job spell and a friend of mine calls me the next day saying where they work is hiring. That would be a synchronicity. Such occurrences are common in magick. For synchronicity to be generated, there needs to be some room for the spell to work in terms of time and circumstance. If you are doing a spell to meet your soulmate, it would be weird to get an invitation to a wedding from a friend you have not seen in years. It is those type of random encounters that may be the way your spell is working towards your goal.

Exercise #79: Self-Enchantment Luck Spell

1. Ground and Cycle Energy.
2. Set your intent. In this case you can use the following statement of intent, "It is my will to become lucky this week, in a way that proves my magick is effective."
3. Open your hand chakras. Imagine energy of luck and good fortune streaming from your hands to outer aura and back to you.
4. Go about your week. If you feel strange pulls or instincts do things you normally would not do (that fall within your normal morality), follow them.
5. Record your result in a magickal journal, or other manner.
6. If desired result is not achieved, repeat.
7. When a spell works, I often feel a tingle and get an intuitive feeling that my spell worked. I also verify my results and see if they fall within my statement of intent.

Spell Tips

Whenever a spell does not work, I ask myself afterwards why it did not work. As a result, or trial and error, here are some lessons I have learned from my failures and successes. Magick is an art and a discipline. It takes practice, and the more you achieve results, the more successful you will typically be.

Be Specific – Be clear with your intentions. The more specific you are typically the better results you get. You also want to get what you really want. Being specific helps you sort and process your desires and solidify your expectations.

Be Honest with Yourself – Put in the magickal energy for what you really need and want. Do not fall into the trap that you are not good enough, magickal enough, or whatever. You are enough.

The Deeper the Trance, the Better the Result – I have gone over this a few times, but it still bears repeating. The deeper your trance is when you do magick, the better the results.

You Get Out What You Put In – The more energy you put into a working the better it will be exponentially. The more I time I take to do a ritual and the more magickal energy I put into it, the better result.

Clear Your Perception Filter – It is alright to ask for what you need and want, and the belief that you are not will get in the way of your magick.

Take Time – Take as much time as you need to have a clear intent, have enough will and energy to summon and direct magickal energy, and plan effectively. There is no rush, unless you are doing emergency magick or direct energy manipulation.

Be Patient – The more difficult and complex the thing is you are trying to manifest, the more time it may take. Doing a working to get a new home, with all the specifics of location, design, etc. you desire – the longer it may take for it to happen. I did a money working and it took over six months for it to bear fruit, but I was able to increase the amount money I brought in.

Work with Energy, Not against It – While you can do any magickal act at any time, sometimes it is best to work with Nature and not against Her. For example, timing spells of prosperity during a waxing or full moon, or doing love spells on a Friday (which is sacred to Venus). This way you are working at least with natural forces, or the egregores of them that people have put stock in over time.

I will go over specific spells in the next chapter – The Energy Magick Grimoire. For now, experiment with your own spells using the above framework and guidelines. I would like to make a differentiation from planned spells to spontaneous ones. Spontaneous magick is necessary, for example, if someone casts an "evil eye" at you, it is best to respond immediately. These direct acts fall more under direct energetic manipulation than formal spell work.

Anatomy of Ritual

I have spoken about the different components of ritual in previous chapters, but in ritual they find a place together. The main pattern can differentiate based upon your personal style and looking at rituals from across a spectrum of influences, they seem to all have similar set ups.

Intent, Research, and Logistics – This is the preliminary step for everything. Have a clear intent and create a statement for it if possible. When you know what your intent is, research how you want the working to take form. It is useful to plan out the actual logistics in the real world. Where is it taking place? Inside or outside? Will you need candles for illumination? Try to think out as many "what ifs" in advance. If you are using a specific metaphysical system, get as much knowledge as you can.

Purification & Banishment – This is to create a clean, neutral environment that is free of energetic contamination. I encourage you to create your own banishing ritual, and if you need more inspiration, please research things such as the Lesser Banishing Ritual of the Pentagram.

Sacred Space & Cosmology – What cosmology you set can affect your workings. The most popular cosmology to cast in Western magick is the four elements and you can also cast the twelve signs of the zodiac, the eight sabbats, the seven chakras, or anything else that is a contained psychic map that accounts for the terrain of the Universe, Time, and Space.

Meditation/Spellwork – This is the heart of the ritual. You could do a guided meditation, a journey, or a spell. How you accomplish your result is as important as the result itself. I find that having everything similarly themed to this point helps with accentuating the magick. For example, for a ritual of empowerment, you might want to evoke the energy of the third chakra to fill your own energetic body to accomplish a difficult task. For that ritual, you might want to evoke the seven chakras in a circle, as if they were elements themselves.

Closing – Thank the beings and energy that you have evoked. Uncast any circles or other constructs. Banish. Purify the space, yourself, and any participants.

That is the basic structure for devising your own spells and rituals. These are more guidelines, and not rules. Your magick should be as flexible as you need. Being stuck in a certain mindset for too long may make the imagination stagnant and imagination is one of the greatest of the practitioner's tools.

Exercise #80: Personal Banishing Ritual

For this ritual, you will need to create a personal banishing sigil and word of power as directed in an earlier chapter.

1. Ground and center in the middle of your chosen ritual area.
2. Take a few steps forward.
3. Draw a personal banishing sigil in the air with energy.
4. Make a banishing tone or use a word of power while you draw the sigil. While you do so, imagine the energy being directed infinitely forward.
5. Walk a quarter circle to the next direction. Repeat Step #4.
6. Repeat Step #5 until you have completed the circle. Make sure you complete the energetic circle.
7. Ground and center.

Exercise #81: Planetary Energy Alignment Ritual

1. As a preliminary step, choose a planet you want to align with and be influenced by.
2. Create sacred space by walking your energetic circle and evoking the seven planets of the ancients- Sun, Moon, Mars, Mercury, Jupiter, Venus, and Saturn- in order as they correspond to the days of the week. If necessary, lay out seven candles in your circle beforehand. Evoke by drawing the sigil for each planet in the air and saying the name of the planet with an intonation.
3. Go to the middle of the circle and trace in energy, the sigil of a planet you choose to align your energy with, in the center of your space. Say words to evoke the planet such

as "I invoke the planet _____ for the purpose of _____."
Or come up with your own.

4. Stand in the sigil and feel the planetary energy course through you. Cycle the energy between the planetary energy in the Heavens, to the sigil on the ground, through the Earth, and back until it is in complete energetic circuit.
5. Center the energy.
6. Step out of the sigil.
7. Banish using your personal banishing ritual.

Ending by banishing is not always necessary, but it avoids having to complete as much energetic purification and it is the most responsible thing to do in spaces that are shared and is a good custom of magickal hygiene.

Of note with ritual, it is important to look at all of the steps as setting the stage for your working. Your intent, every word, and every action helps set the stage and build upon the experience. Choose care in what you put together, and feel free to experiment and refine. There is very little that cannot be fixed in your personal practice with banishing, grounding, centering, and rest.

Part III
The Energy Magick Grimoire

Chapter 13

The Energy Magick Grimoire

Summary: Balance, Defense, Healing, Love, Miscellaneous, Offense, Prosperity, Protection, Self-Empowerment, Shadow Work, and Spiritual Evolution

The following is an energetic grimoire of spells and techniques to accomplish your goals. I am not quantifying magick into "black" and "white" categories, and some spells that are in the offensive category may fall into defensive, and vice versa. Sometimes you must do what you have to do. Sometimes the "higher path" is a luxury. Ideally, magick should be used to better yourself, your situation in life, and your spiritual development.

The topics are arranged in alphabetical order and draw from several of the exercises from above. Think of them more as magickal recipes instead of exercises. You can change them to more specific situations as need be, just as you might modify the ingredients of a culinary recipe.

In some cases, I will use energy directly, and in others I will use energy in coordination with standard practices of witchcraft. For each category, I will do at least three separate exercises for each category to get a feel for examples of what you can do.

Before and after every working, I would purify, ground, and center. This does a couple of things. First, it gets you back to "reality". Secondly, we want to avoid "lust of result" and have a nice beginning and end to every working to seal the working and allow the energy to do its thing without further influence or energetic contamination.

Enjoy yourself. The more relaxed you are when you do magick, the better it works.

Balance

I have found that I am a better practitioner and Pagan when I seek balance and harmony – both within and outside of myself. The real challenge is to stay balanced in a chaotic world. There is a lot of distraction, and a lot of things demanding your attention. When I need a reset, or when I need to find that sense of harmony I lost, I go back to some of the techniques below.

Two of Pentacles Exercise

This exercise is designed to create balance in separate parts of one's life that are in conflict. For example, sometimes I have a problem balancing work and home life. It draws inspiration for the Two of Pentacles card in tarot – which is typically a card inviting someone to find balance in their lives – and is also useful in balancing two different forces and is like the exercise in holding energetic paradox. It is also a useful exercise if you are indecisive like I am sometimes, and you cannot choose between two life altering choices.

1. Get into a state of meditation.
2. Make an energy ball.
3. Imagine that in this ball is one aspect of your life that you are trying to resolve.
4. Make a second energy ball in your other hand – imagine the part of your life that is in conflict with the first.
5. Make both balls overlap. Imagine there are cords connecting both balls to your center.
6. Absorb both balls and cords into your center.
7. Sit in meditation. If needed, open your third eye to channel inspiration on how to move forward in your life.
8. Ground and journal any images, thoughts, or inspirations that are revealed.

Kabbalistic Pillar Exercise

This was an exercise one of my first teachers liked to employ to help me find balance and peace. It is inspired by the Kabbalistic pillars in the Western Mystery Tradition.

1. Stand in a quiet place. Close your eyes.
2. Imagine you are standing between two pillars – one white and one black. On your left is a white pillar symbolizing strength and power. On your right is a black pillar of mercy and compassion.
3. Open your hand chakras and feel both pillars as if they were physical.
4. Slowly fold your arms over your chest.
5. Feel and visualize that you are standing within a middle pillar. The more you feel and stand in the pillar, imagine, and feel your energy becoming more balanced.
6. Rest in the feeling of balance.
7. When you are ready, open your eyes and imagine the pillars fading.

Cycling between Moon and Earth

I love the moon, and I feel that since the moon rules emotions, the more we connect with the moon and their cycles, the more emotional balance we can acquire. This exercise also serves to gain more awareness of lunar cycles. I like to start this at the waxing crescent so that I have a nice visual representation of the moon in the sky, but you can start at the new moon as well. If starting at the new moon, do your best to be aware of the position as much as possible.

1. At waxing crescent moon phase (go outside if you are able), meditate on the moon's position in the sky (sitting or standing).

2. Slowly breathe in the energy of the moon and breathe it out through your body to the Earth.
3. Bring the energy to the center of the Earth.
4. Breathe in Earth energy, hold it in your body, exhale to the Moon.
5. Inhale from the Moon, hold the energy, and feel yourself consumed by it. Breathe out through your body to the Earth.
6. Keep repeating this pattern.
7. When you are ready, center the energy, and resume regular breathing.
8. Repeat for each moon phase – so full moon, waxing crescent, new moon, and so on.

Defense

These are spells and methods for magickal defense. People will throw energy at you – whether you like it or not. I am not saying everyone is trying to psychically attack you, but even the energy of non-practitioners can affect you dramatically. Defense is sometimes needed to be enacted as a coping mechanism for everyday life until you can make changes (for example, having toxic family members or toxic co-workers).

Warding Off the Evil Eye

When someone looks at you in the eye and is sending negative energy through sight, it is easy to thwart it through the following method. You are catching and releasing any negative energy thrown at you. This can be performed in any situation you feel that someone is casting negative energy in your direction.

1. Make a mudra, with the hand closest to the person casting the "evil eye", with your thumb holding down your middle and ring fingers together.
2. Catch the energy between your index and little fingers.

3. Release the energy and dispose of it to the Earth to be recycled.

Creating a Defensive Alchemical Energy Construct

This technique combines creating thought forms with alchemy. The more energy that is thrown at you, the stronger you become. I created this exercise so that it empowers you physically, but if you want it to empower any other part of your life, just switch it from going to root chakra to another chakra.

1. Summon a classic energy ball. Shape it into a cube.
2. Make the side facing away from you the "input" side that takes in energy from the outside.
3. Make the side facing towards you an "output" side.
4. Make a cord connecting the "output" side to your root chakra.
5. Program the cube with the four stages of alchemy so that any energy coming in is "burned" of its information, purified, blessed, and transformed to be taken in.
6. Program the cube to take a small part of energy for its maintenance with the majority going to you via the chakra cord you created.
7. Turn the cube on. You can will it to happen, or even make an energetic switch.
8. Place the cube somewhere above and to the side of you, just outside your outer aura. Perform maintenance on the cube as necessary.

The Mirrored Shield

This working involves some energetic mechanics of using your shield as a base, removing it, and transferring it to make a temporary shield that keeps a toxic person's energy directed towards them. This works better than simply creating a mirrored shield around someone since you have "incubated" it.

1. Make two new energy shields.
2. See, feel, and imagine the outer shield becoming a mirrored dome that surrounds you. The longer you hold it and use the shield, the stronger the effect (I recommend at least an hour, but 1-2 days is optimal).
3. When you are near the toxic person. See, feel, and imagine your shield peeling off of you and onto them – with the mirror side pointed towards the target.
4. Seal the mirrored shield energetically.
5. Cut any cords between you and the mirrored shield.

Healing

With most energy healing, I recommend it for direct application in person, but there are more than a few techniques for helping people out from a distance.

Distance Sigil Healing

While energy is not confined to time or space in many ways, I find it satisfying to send energy directly to those in need.

1. Make a statement of intent for someone to be healed.
2. Create a sigil and a word of power out of the statement.
3. As you make the sigil in the air energetically, imagine it is a portal sending the healing energies to the target directly – letting the energy go where it needs to.
4. Focus on sending healing.
5. When done, close the portal and banish the sigil.

Past Life Healing

Energetic cords connect us to not only others, but to ourselves – even our past selves. The goal of this working is to heal wounds from the past that we cannot get to easily. If you want to go to some other life, or explore those connections, make that clear in any opening intent.

1. Center.
2. Astral project to a neutral place, then change the place to become a comfortable, dark space that you feel relaxed in. This is a time outside of time. A place outside of place.
3. Make the intent of feeling the cord that connects you from this life to your last. This should come from your center.
4. Feel for the cord and visualize in your mind's eye what it is connected to. It may be another person, or a globe of light. This is a representation of your past self.
5. Feel the cord, analyze it, and see where it needs healing. Visualize the cord as made of light and look for any dark spots indicating healing that needs to occur.
6. Heal the cord with light.
7. Be aware of what is on the other end of the cord, bring it to focus, and then bring it in front of you.
8. If the energy comes as a person, imagine that person in front of you. Do a diagnosis of where they need healing and apply healing energy. If it is something else, imagine it's astral double made of light, and do any necessary healing work.
9. Project back to your body.
10. Banish as needed.

Healing the Energetic Double

This one is a little tricky. You will have to journey to the Underworld, find the energetic double of the person that needs healing, then travel back. I would bring a guide of an ally with you, which could be a living, breathing person or spiritual entities.

1. Get into trance. Get as deep as you can.
2. Journey and travel to the Underworld. You can fly, ride a spirit animal, or any other manner.
3. The Underworld is like the astral in many ways. Imagine you are traveling to the Underworld through a tunnel.

4. When you arrive at the Underworld, if there is a guardian, negotiate with respect if necessary.
5. Make the intention that your path will be clear. Follow the path to the energetic double of the person who needs healing.
6. Apply healing energy to their double.
7. When done, make the intention for a path going back to where you came.
8. Exit the Underworld, thank your allies and guides.

Love

Love magick is tricky. Here is a story for you. A person uses a love spell to get a certain guy they were infatuated with. The guy returns her feelings. The guy gets obsessed with her. The guy then gets horribly jealous because of the obsession. The guy becomes abusive towards the person who casts the love spell. This is not an unusual situation with love spells. I advocate magick to enhance self-love or workings to express and enhance love. Manipulating people with magick eventually comes back to take its revenge. Besides, isn't it better that you know someone actually has feelings for you instead of coercing them into it with magick?

Basic Glamour

Glamour magick is all about perception, and the most important person you need to impress is yourself. When I have done glamour, I have done it out of a place of lack of self-esteem. I wanted to be adored and have people feel like I was important. I realized that the reason I was doing all of this was out of some internal lack on my part. I needed to be special. When I do glamour, it is mostly for me. I want to see that specialness reflected back at me in a healthy way so I can remember to love myself. Glamour is also good for when you need to make an impression, like a job interview.

1. Go to a mirror.
2. Focus on the part of your body that you want to change the perception of and send it energy.
3. Imagine that part of your body radiating the power of attraction.
4. Focus on the energy where that body part is and feel it – let that energy of beauty spread to the rest of your body.
5. Keep the energy in place with your intention and banish when complete.
6. Variations include keying your glamour to a word of power, so that you can call it up quickly; or focusing on a body part you already find attractive and start from there.

The Twin Blossom Chakras

This is for two or more people to work with. This is an intimate exchange of energy and should only be done to further enhance a relationship that is already present. Sit across for the person you are in a relationship with.

1. Focus on your root chakra, imagine energy coming from your root, going out of your body, to their root chakra. Have the other person visualize and feel this energy. Bring both of your attention to the energy that is being transferred.
2. Have the other person send out that energy from their root to your second chakra. Breathe in the energy to your second chakra. Hold the energy and send it to their second chakra. When either person holds the energy, do it for a few breaths at minimum.
3. Have the other person hold the energy, then send it from their second chakra to your solar plexus chakra.
4. Keep repeating this process until there is connection between both people's crown chakra.
5. Both of you should focus on the energetic connection. Match breathing, if possible.

6. Focus on your root chakra opening like a flower, have your partner do the same.
7. Slowly go up the chakras, blossoming each one in sync as much as possible (this may take some extra communication).
8. When you reach the crown, let your crown chakras overlap. Breathe in the divine energy together. Rest in that harmony between the both of you and the Universe, spirits, the gods, etc.
9. Slowly close your chakras back.
10. Each person should center.
11. Open eyes if they are closed.

Miscellaneous

These are spells and techniques that do not follow other categories. The results and intentions do vary.

The Crucible

Change is inevitable and I have had times where I get stuck in life and need to initiate change. Alchemy is the occult science of change. Physical alchemist would often use a crucible to heat something to extreme temperatures. This working is inspired by those alchemists and uses the 4-step process of alchemy. The intent is purification and renewal. Spend at least 5 minutes in each stage.

1. Cast an energetic triangle. Sit within it.
2. Imagine the triangle is filling with black flame. Let it burn away your thoughts and clear your mind.
3. See and feel white light fill the pyramid. Let the light purify you from the top down, grounding the energy into the Earth.

4. Visualize and feel a gold light descending upon you – the light of Spirit, the gods, and your Higher Power. Let the light bless you and fill you with sacredness and peace.
5. Lastly, visualize the pyramid being completely filled with red light – the light of personal strength and power. Let the light fill your entire astral body. As you breathe in the energy, feel your vitality fill as much as possible.
6. Ground any excess energy as you wish. Banish the triangle from within it.

Third Eye Enhancement

Typically for divination, I will use tarot, pendulum, runes, or some other method. The third eye is the seat of intuition and powers any divinatory work I do. The below method enhances your intuition and opens the "pipe" between you and the Divine a little more. I recommend charging your divination tools to give them a little extra energetic help. Banish and purify your space. Sit in meditation.

1. Open your hand chakras. Place one hand over your third eye.
2. Open your third eye as you send energy to it with the hand covering it.
3. Open your crown chakra. Send energy through your third eye to your crown chakra and through it. Remove your hand from your forehead.
4. As you breathe in, breathe in through the crown and out through the third eye.
5. Imagine your third eye as open as possible,
6. Do divination with your chosen method.
7. Close your third eye and crown.
8. Ground.

Group Thought Form

This technique can be used for any purpose. Create your intent as a group. There is a certain magick when people create and do magick together. This builds on that knowledge.

1. Set your intent.
2. Purify the space and create sacred space.
3. Hold hands and imagine a portal in the middle. This portal is opening from the accumulation of your combined mind space.
4. Imagine the thought form rising from the portal.
5. Give the thought form a name, a purpose, and a timeframe. Ask the thought form to disperse from where it came when its job has been accomplished.
6. Chant a word of power, or a phrase of intent continuously until the energy climaxes. All energy raised goes to the thought form.
7. Tell the thought form to do its work. Feel and imagine it leaving under its own power to accomplish the task.
8. Close the portal. Release hands.
9. Banish, purify, ground as needed.

Evocation of a Plant Spirit

This technique can be used for any purpose as it corresponds to the plant you are using. You could use cinnamon for prosperity, angelica for banishment, mugwort to assist you in dreams or spiritual journeying, etc. As preliminary work, research the plant's medicinal and magickal properties (including planetary correspondences). You can work with the plant ritually as appropriate. If it is safe to, burn it as incense or take it into yourself by making and drinking a tea.

1. Purify the space and create sacred space. You can draw in the planetary energy that corresponds to the plant.

2. Create the protective circle, triangle of manifestation, and a portal between us and the realm of plant allies.
3. Put the herb you are working with in the triangle.
4. Evoke the plant spirit by name.
5. Burn incense or make tea.
6. Follow the steps as outlined above for evocation.

Offense

I typically take a philosophy of aikido where I like to resolve conflict as safely, quickly, and peacefully as possible. Sometimes you do need to assert your boundaries, take actions for self-defense, or even "banish with extreme prejudice" as an old friend of mine would say. The following techniques allow the practitioner to strike to resolve conflicts.

The Astral Egg

This borders between offense and defense. The magickal theory here is based on sympathetic magick, where what you do to representation of someone will happen to the person themselves. This technique is to take an astral poppet of the person bothering you and put them in a mirrored egg where they can cause less trouble. The person in the egg will feel trapped, claustrophobic, and impotent. It is advisable to take the person out of the egg when they are no longer a problem, but many times the egg will fade naturally.

1. Astral project to a neutral place of your choosing. From there journey to what you imagine is an empty place. Let the place become white and infinite.
2. Think of the person that is troubling you. Gather energy to make a small representation of them. Place this person in the "middle" of the place.
3. Form an energetic egg around the representation of the person. Imagine it as a flat disk underneath them that gradually turns in to an egg that surrounds them.

4. Seal the egg with a predetermined phrase of your choosing, statement of intent, or word of power.
5. Cut any cords connecting you to that person and the energetic representation of them.
6. Journey back to your neutral space and then back to your body.

The Magickal Dart

When you need to directly affect a situation and end a conflict – this is the way. I use these in extreme situations. This is like having a loaded gun and I recommend that you treat this working as the weapons it is. There are also variations on the technique, that I will write below. The dart pierces the aura and can go deep into the target's energy body.

1. Form energy in your projective hand in a ball or any other shape.
2. Put as much energy and emotion into that shape.
3. Feel and transform the shape into something that looks kind of pointy and sharp.
4. Cut the cord between you and the energy dart.
5. Throw the energetic dart at your target. Imaging it is piercing their aura and hitting straight into their energetic body.
6. Banish, purify, ground, and center.

Variations include the chakra dart that targets a particular chakra (for example, into the throat chakra of someone spreading gossip about you); darts that dissolve and poison the energetic system of the target; and darts that are thought forms that will transform inside the target's energy and accomplish a specific task.

Offensive Cord Cutting

This is not really a technique, but more of a way of using an earlier technique offensively. I talked a lot about cutting your own cords in a previous chapter, but this is to cut someone else's cords. This should not be done lightly. An example where I would feel justified is if one of my kid's was being threatened and I needed to cut the connection between my child and someone hurtful. While someone might be tempted to use this technique to break people up, keep in mind that people in a relationship that are attracted to each other will re-grow cords (trust me on this one).

1. State your intent.
2. See in your mind's eye and imagine the two people that have a connection you want to cut.
3. Imagine that this is their connection in the astral.
4. Reach "up" into the astral to feel their cords.
5. Make an energetic weapon to cut the cords. Cut the cord as close as possible to the first person, and then grabbing the dangling cord with the other hand, cut as close as possible to the second person.
6. Discard of the cords in your hand.
7. Reach closer to your body, close any astral portal formed (and there more than likely is).

Prosperity

Making changes in our finances has been the goal of magick since practitioners have been doing it. Part of what makes prosperity magick difficult is accepting the fact that you are worthy of prosperity. While immediate financial windfalls can happen, I prefer to work on gradual improvements of finances that are measurable. In general, I find that gradual process for long term goals raises the self-esteem of the practitioner and raises confidence.

Prosperity Poppet

This working needs to have your intent clear for what you want in life. This is a long-term working. It is good for self-love as much as it is for prosperity.

1. Create an intent to meet all your needs and desires.
2. Astral project to a neutral place, then create or journey to a place where there is large room with a doll house. This doll house should be a recreation of where you live.
3. Transform the doll house to your ideal home. Create everything that you desire.
4. While projecting, make poppet made of energy. Make it as exact as possible.
5. Animate the poppet and have it live in its home.
6. Make a protective shield around the poppet and its home.
7. Visit the poppet monthly. Do any energetic maintenance. Change if needed.

Money Enchantment Spell

This spell is good for an increase in money over time. You can use paper money, a bank card, or your wallet.

1. Have the clear intention that whatever money you put out will come back to you greater.
2. Create a key word or use a word of power that connects with your intent.
3. Hold some paper money or your bank card and enchant them with the energy of your intention.
4. Whenever you use that money or your bank card, say or clearly think that key word.

Boomerang Object Spell

Sometimes prosperity is keeping what we have and not losing what we have worked hard for. The following is an object enchantment to keep your stuff close, prevent you from losing it, or getting back what you have lost. You will have to create a personal sigil for this working. To make a personal sigil, take all the unique letters of your name and arrange them in a design as you would with any other sigil using the reduction method.

1. Make an intent clear that the object you possess is yours and will remain yours.
2. Hold the object to want to enchant in one hand.
3. With the other hand, touch the energetic area of your root chakra and make a cord that connects your root to the object.
4. Repeat for each chakra or as many feels right.

Prosperity Bind Rune Ritual

You will need some research and at least four people to do this working. Bind runes are combination of runes created for specific effects. This one uses the runes of Fehu (wealth), Othala (family wealth), Gebo (gift), and Algiz (protection, but in this case protecting and keeping your wealth). Research the runes beforehand and arrange them into a single symbol that each person memorizes. Something like what is pictured will work, but you can arrange your own.

1. Solidify your intent for prosperity and wealth.
2. Create sacred space.
3. Arrange everyone so that they are in a circle and equidistant from each other. Beforehand, each person chooses one of the four main runes to sing.
4. Hold hands.
5. Have the person singing Fehu go first, then everyone joins in gradually.
6. Each person should be singing their rune at the same time.
7. While singing, see, feel, and imagine, the bind rune in the middle of the circle.
8. Keep singing until it reaches a climax. Hold the energetic bind rune in the middle.
9. Feel the bind rune radiate to and through each person, including yourself.
10. Send the bind rune to the Heavens with your intentions.
11. Banish, purify, and ground, as needed.

Protection

Protection is slightly different from defensive magick, in the sense that it is pro-active and not reactive. I think it is safe to employ protection magick for many situations. It is like insurance – better to have it and not need it, than to need it and not have it.

Protection from the Elements

This is a petitionary working, where you are asking for protection from the elements. I would re-do this every year. Perhaps make it part of a spring tradition.

1. Make a statement of intent for each element. Something like "It is my will, that I be protected from the element of _____, all of it spirits, and all that it is made from _____."

2. Make four triangles of manifestation, one for each quarter.
3. Cast a protective circle in the middle, between the triangles, but giving enough space between them.
4. In the east, call upon the spirits of Air. Open the portal to the elemental realm of that quarter.
5. Speak the statement of intent for each element.
6. Offer something to each element such as incense for air, a candle for fire, etc. or it could be a libation to each.
7. Thank the spirits.
8. Close the portals, banish, purify, and ground.

Wards of Saturn

I use these to ward off unwelcome visitors, and it really shows me what people intend or how they might affect me. These energetic wards are put at the corner of your home. The intention is that the wards will stop people that mean you harm from coming to your home. Alternatively, if you let in people into your home that you thought were safe, but they mean you harm, those people will get very uncomfortable and leave. This should be repeated monthly, and the more you do it, the more effective it will be since you will layering energetic wards upon wards.

1. Make your intentions clear to match the purpose of the spell.
2. Make a large energy ball, fill it with the energy of Saturn.
3. Use your intention and will to focus the energy while you make a gesture of sending that energy to each specific corner of your home.
4. Repeat for each corner (at least 8).

Car Protection

Your objects can be shielded just like you can. I use this technique to protect vehicles.

1. Get a ball of energy and make it into a thought form that will warn you of impending danger.
2. Shape the energy into a hood ornament and install on your vehicle.
3. Make an energetic shield around your car with the intention of protecting it from accidents. This should be done clockwise.
4. Make the shield three times, as you circle the vehicle you make a new layer.
5. Condense the shield as much as possible, paying attention to the early warning thought form hood ornament.
6. Do a layer of invisibility (I do this since I speed sometimes, and I like extra protection if I do).

Self-Empowerment, Shadow Work, and Spiritual Evolution

All three of these subjects blend together. Self-empowerment comes from knowing the self. Shadow work is necessary to know every aspect of yourself and to heal the self. Spiritual evolution and growth come from being empowered to constantly grow and change for the better – to heal the wounds of the self and grow into something greater than what we were before.

Evocation of the Shadow

Of all the techniques here, I can honestly say this one saved my life. I have not always been the best person, and I was acting from a place of woundedness and pain for a long time. The evocation of my shadow allowed me to literally come face to face with my demons. The shadow self is the part of us that is hidden, repressed, or denied by the conscious self. A lot of pain, but also personal power, can be wrapped up inside of it. While some people may try to face and reconcile with their entire shadow self, the following technique is used to face it piece by piece. This can be done with physical or astral evocation.

Steps 1 through 4 must be taken care of in one sitting, while steps 5 through 7 can happen at your own pace.

1. Confrontation/Inventory: Make a list of your negative aspects or traumas that you are trying to face. This first step can be difficult since it is a conscious and willing step into opening parts of yourself that may be painful. After you make the list, choose one that you want to deal with right now – choosing the least troubling thing first. Keep the list, as it will be useful to go back to in order to deal with more of what is troubling you.

2. Emotional Purge: Get out your emotions as much as you can about the thing you have chosen. Write it out, or use art, or even just screaming, yelling, or crying. Do everything you can to get those emotions out.

3. Emotional Separation: Imagine those emotions floating away from you and collecting in a space. This can be an imaginary place, or even just a blank void. Imagine those coming away from and collecting into something like a cloud that is separate from you.

4. Thoughtform Creation: Give your thought form shape. What color is it? What does it look like? What does its voice sound like? How many arms, legs, eyes, etc., does it have? Finally, ask it what its name is.

5. Making Friends: Take time to meditate on the creature you have created. Talk to it. Ask it questions. Treat it as you would a new friend you are getting to know. Remember this creature is a part of yourself. It cannot hurt you. It is made of your emotions and your programming that helped you deal with negative or traumatic things that happened in your life.

6. Discovery: Ask your shadow creature what purpose it had in your life. Learn from it. Realize that it no longer needs to be in your life.

7. Reconciliation: Thank your shadow creature, and either visualize a portal for it to leave or if you are comfortable with the idea – hug it good-bye and let it flow back into you.

After Step 7 take time to recover, relax, and soothe yourself. You did a lot of hard work that not a lot of people can do. Be proud of this. Repeat the steps as much as you can, working on harder aspects as you continue.

Cutting Cords with the Past

This technique is good when you feel you are completely different person from who you were in the past. The purpose is to move on. I found it difficult to move on from who I was at one point, and this technique can help you find some sense of closure.

1. Sit in meditation.
2. Astral project to a place that is not a place. A time that is not a time. Go to a neutral space that is completely empty.
3. Journey to this place until you find your past self. If necessary, create a portal to go through.
4. Talk to your past self and tell them what they mean to you and how you need to move on.
5. Visualize the cords between the both of you. Slowly cut them one by one.
6. Thank your past self. Come back to your body.
7. Perform energetic healing on where you cut the cords.
8. Rest and do aftercare.

Merging with the Wisdom Self

We are made of many parts. If time and space are just illusions, then the people we want to be – the people we evolve into – are just within reach. This spell can be repeated as necessary.

While you cannot merge completely with your "future" self, you can be influenced by them, and they can help you see your spiritual path a little more clearly.

1. Get into trance by way of dancing.
2. As you get deeper into trance, let your chakras open one by one from root to crown.
3. Continue going as deep as you can into trance.
4. Imagine that behind or beside you there is someone else dancing next to you. Imagine and feel that this person is a wiser, stronger version of you.
5. Dance in synch with your future self.
6. Make a step closer to them and have them take a step towards you until you are overlapping.
7. Dance as one being. Make note of how you feel.
8. Take a step back to your original position and allow your future self to do the same.
9. Slow down your dancing, and let your awareness come back to the present.
10. Ground and center as needed.

Final Note

I hope these spells and techniques serve you well, and that you have enjoyed this work. While I am not responsible for any work of magick you do by yourself, I do feel some responsibility for presenting the information. As such, if you need help or have any questions, I am available via social media and my website marknecampjr.com. I am always happy to clarify or explain something.

Lastly, I leave you with a prayer:

May you clear away the wreckage of the past and embrace a new destiny.
When your life is at its darkest, realize what a light you are.
May the gods and ancestors bless you and keep you.
May your grow strong and wise, and may good fortune only be just a little magick away from you.

Blessings,
Mark NeCamp, Jr.

Bibliography

Andrews, Ted. *Animal Speak*. Llewellyn Worldwide, 2010.

—. *The Healer's Manual*. Llewellyn Worldwide, 1993.

Aoumiel, and Ann Moura. *Grimoire for the Green Witch*. Llewellyn Worldwide, 2003.

Bartlett, Robert Allen. *Real Alchemy*. Nicolas-Hays, Inc., 2009.

Bek, Lilla, and Philippa Pullar. *Healing with Chakra Energy*. Destiny Books, 1995.

Bennett-Goleman, Tara. *Emotional Alchemy*. Harmony, 2002.

Brannen, Cyndi. *True Magic*. John Hunt Publishing, 2019.

Buckland, Raymond. *Buckland's Complete Book of Witchcraft*. Llewellyn Worldwide, 1986.

Carroll, Peter J. *Liber Null & Psychonaut*. Weiser Books, 1987.

Carse, James. *Finite and Infinite Games*. Simon and Schuster, 2011.

Cicero, Chic, and Sandra Tabatha Cicero. *The Essential Golden Dawn*. Llewellyn Worldwide, 2003.

Coddington, Mary. *Seekers of the Healing Energy*. Inner Traditions / Bear & Co, 1991.

Conley, Craig. *Magic Words*. Weiser Books, 2008.

Couliano, Ioan P. *Eros and Magic in the Renaissance*. University of Chicago Press, 1987.

Cunningham, Scott. *Divination for Beginners*. Llewellyn Worldwide Limited, 2003.

—. *Wicca*. Llewellyn Worldwide, 2010.

Denning, Melita, and Osborne Phillips. *Planetary Magick*. Llewellyn Worldwide, 2011.

Easwaran, Eknath. *How to Meditate*. Nilgiri Press, 2011.

Farrell, Nick. *Making Talismans*. Llewellyn Worldwide, 2001.

Forrest, Steven. *The Inner Sky*. Seven Paws PressInc, 2012.

Fortune, Dion. *Applied Magic*. Weiser Books, 2000.

—. *Aspects of Occultism*. Weiser Books, 2000.

—. *Psychic Self-Defense*. Weiser Books, 2020.

Goldberg, Bruce. *Astral Voyages*. Llewellyn Worldwide, 1999.

Goodman, Felicitas D. *Where the Spirits Ride the Wind*. Indiana University Press, 1990.

Goodman, Felicitas D., and Nana Nauwald. *Ecstatic Trance*. Binkey Kok, Holland, 2003.

Greer, John Michael. *Circles of Power*. Llewellyn Worldwide, 1997.

—. *Paths of Wisdom*. Thoth, 2007.

—. *The Occult Book*. Sterling, 2017.

Greer, Mary K. K. *Archetypal Tarot*. Red Wheel/Weiser, 2021.

Hauck, Dennis William. *The Emerald Tablet*. Penguin, 1999.

Hine, Phil. *Condensed Chaos*. Original Falcon Press, 2009.

Hope, Murry. *The Psychology of Ritual*. Element Books Limited, 1988.

Hulse, David Allen. *The Eastern Mysteries*. Llewellyn Worldwide, 2000.

—. *The Western Mysteries*. Llewellyn Publications, 2000.

Illes, Judika. *Encyclopedia of 5,000 Spells*. Harper Collins, 2011.

—. *Encyclopedia of Spirits*. Harper Collins, 2010.

Initiates, Three. *The Kybalion: Centenary Edition*. Penguin, 2018.

Judith, Anodea. *Eastern Body, Western Mind*. Clarkson Potter, 2004.

—. *Wheels of Life*. Llewellyn Worldwide Limited, 1999.

K, Amber. *Covencraft*. Llewellyn Worldwide, 1998.

—. *True Magick*. Llewellyn Worldwide, 2006.

Konstantinos. *Summoning Spirits*. Llewellyn Worldwide Limited, 2002.

Kraig, Donald Michael. *Modern Magick*. Llewellyn Worldwide, 2010.

—. *Tarot and Magic*. Llewellyn Worldwide Limited, 2002.

Leadbeater, Charles Webster. *The Inner Life*. Sirius-C Media, 2017.

Mann, A. T. *The Mandala Astrological Tarot*. Sterling Publishing Company Incorporated, 2009.

Mann, Ronald L. *Sacred Healing*. Blue Dolphin Pub, 1998.

McQuillar, Tayannah Lee. *Astrology for Mystics*. Simon and Schuster, 2021.

Moura, Ann. *Green Witchcraft*. Llewellyn Worldwide, 2014.

Nettesheim, Heinrich Cornelius Agrippa. *Three Books of Occult Philosophy*. Llewellyn Worldwide, 1993.

Ophiel. *The Art and Practice of Astral Projection*. Weiser Books, 1974.

Paulson, Genevieve Lewis. *Kundalini and the Chakras*. Llewellyn Worldwide, 2004.

Paxson, Diana L. *Taking Up the Runes*. Red Wheel/Weiser, 2021.

Paxson, Diana L. *Trance-Portation*. Weiser Books, 2008.

Pirsig, Robert M. *Zen and the Art of Motorcycle Maintenance*. Harper Collins, 2009.

Ramacharaka, Yogi. *Fourteen Lessons in Yogi Philosophy and Oriental Occultism (Classic Reprint)*. Forgotten Books, 2017.

—. *Science of Breath*. Yoga Publications Society, 1905.

Roth, Gabrielle, and John Loudon. *Maps to Ecstasy*. New World Library, 1998.

Shesso, Renna. *Math for Mystics*. Weiser Books, 2007.

Simpson, Liz. *The Book of Chakra Healing*. Sterling Publishing Company, Inc., 1999.

Spare, Austin Osman, and Jake Dirnberger. *The Pocket Austin Osman Spare*. Trident Business Partners, 2020.

Starhawk. *Spiral Dance, The – 20th Anniversary*. Harper Collins, 1999.

Stavish, Mark. *Egregores*. Inner Traditions, 2018.

The Cloud of Unknowing and Other Works. Penguin UK, 2001.

Tyson, Donald. *The Magician's Workbook*. Llewellyn Worldwide, 2001.

Tyson, Jenny. *The Art of Scrying and Dowsing*. Llewellyn Publications, 2021.

Vayne, Julian, and Greg Humphries. *Now That's What I Call Chaos Magick*. Mandrake, 2005.

Versluis, Arthur. *The Philosophy of Magic*. Arkana, 1988.

Waite, Arthur Edward. *The Pictorial Key to the Tarot*. Weiser Books, 1975.

Whitcomb, Bill. *The Magician's Companion*. Llewellyn Worldwide, 1993.

(Witch), Lisa Chamberlain. *Runes for Beginners*. 2018.

Woolfold, Joanna Martine. *The Only Astrology Book You'll Ever Need*. Taylor Trade Publications, 2008.

Zell-Ravenheart, Oberon, and Morning Glory Zell-Ravenheart. *Creating Circles and Ceremonies*. Career Press, 2006.

MOON BOOKS
PAGANISM & SHAMANISM

What is Paganism? A religion, a spirituality, an alternative belief system, nature worship? You can find support for all these definitions (and many more) in dictionaries, encyclopaedias, and text books of religion, but subscribe to any one and the truth will evade you. Above all Paganism is a creative pursuit, an encounter with reality, an exploration of meaning and an expression of the soul. Druids, Heathens, Wiccans and others, all contribute their insights and literary riches to the Pagan tradition. Moon Books invites you to begin or to deepen your own encounter, right here, right now.

If you have enjoyed this book, why not tell other readers by posting a review on your preferred book site.

Bestsellers from Moon Books
Pagan Portals Series

The Morrigan
Meeting the Great Queens
Morgan Daimler
Ancient and enigmatic, the Morrigan reaches out to us.
On shadowed wings and in raven's call, meet the ancient Irish
goddess of war, battle, prophecy, death, sovereignty, and magic.
Paperback: 978-1-78279-833-0 ebook: 978-1-78279-834-7

The Awen Alone
Walking the Path of the Solitary Druid
Joanna van der Hoeven
An introductory guide for the solitary Druid, The Awen Alone will
accompany you as you explore, and seek out your own place
within the natural world.
Paperback: 978-1-78279-547-6 ebook: 978-1-78279-546-9

Moon Magic
Rachel Patterson
An introduction to working with the phases of the Moon,
what they are and how to live in harmony with the lunar
year and to utilise all the magical powers it provides.
Paperback: 978-1-78279-281-9 ebook: 978-1-78279-282-6

Hekate
A Devotional
Vivienne Moss
Hekate, Queen of Witches and the Shadow-Lands,
haunts the pages of this devotional bringing magic
and enchantment into your lives.
Paperback: 978-1-78535-161-7 ebook: 978-1-78535-162-4

Readers of ebooks can buy or view any of these bestsellers by clicking on the live link in the title. Most titles are published in paperback and as an ebook. Paperbacks are available in traditional bookshops. Both print and ebook formats are available online.

Find more titles and sign up to our readers' newsletter http://www.johnhuntpublishing.com/paganism

For video content, author interviews and more, please subscribe to our YouTube channel.

MoonBooksPublishing

Follow us on social media for book news, promotions and more:

Facebook: Moon Books Publishing

Instagram: @moonbooksjhp

Twitter: @MoonBooksJHP

Tik Tok: @moonbooksjhp